Cooperation and Competition
in a Common Market

Contributions to Economics

Sabine Spangenberg
The Institutionalised Transformation of the East German Economy
1998. ISBN 3-7908-1103-3

Hagen Bobzin
Indivisibilities
1998. ISBN 3-7908-1123-8

Helmut Wagner (Ed.)
Current Issues in Monetary Economics
1998. ISBN 3-7908-1127-0

Peter Michaelis/Frank Stähler (Eds.)
Recent Policy Issues in Environmental and Resource Economics
1998. ISBN 3-7908-1137-8

Jessica de Wolff
The Political Economy of Fiscal Decisions
1998. ISBN 3-7908-1130-0

Georg Bol/Gholamreza Nakhaeizadeh/ Karl-Heinz Vollmer (Eds.)
Risk Measurements, Econometrics and Neural Networks
1998. ISBN 3-7908-1152-1

Joachim Winter
Investment and Exit Decisions at the Plant Level
1998. ISBN 3-7908-1154-8

Bernd Meyer
Intertemporal Asset Pricing
1999. ISBN 3-7908-1159-9

Uwe Walz
Dynamics of Regional Integration
1999. ISBN 3-7908-1185-8

Michael Carlberg
European Monetary Union
1999. ISBN 3-7908-1191-2

Giovanni Galizzi/ Luciano Venturini (Eds.)
Vertical Relationships and Coordination in the Food System
1999. ISBN 3-7908-1192-0

Gustav A. Horn/Wolfgang Scheremet/ Rudolf Zwiener
Wages and the Euro
1999. ISBN 3-7908-1199-8

Dirk Willer
The Development of Equity Capital Markets in Transition Economies
1999. ISBN 3-7908-1198-X

Karl Matthias Weber
Innovation Diffusion and Political Control of Energy Technologies
1999. ISBN 3-7908-1205-6

Heike Link et al.
The Costs of Road Infrastructure and Congestion in Europe
1999. ISBN 3-7908-1201-3

Simon Duindam
Military Conscription
1999. ISBN 3-7908-1203-X

Bruno Jeitziner
Political Economy of the Swiss National Bank
1999. ISBN 3-7908-1209-9

Irene Ring et al. (Eds.)
Regional Sustainability
1999. ISBN 3-7908-1233-1

Katharina Müller/Andreas Ryll/ Hans-Jürgen Wagener (Eds.)
Transformation of Social Security: Pensions in Central-Eastern Europe
1999. ISBN 3-7908-1210-2

Stefan Traub
Framing Effects in Taxation
1999. ISBN 3-7908-1240-4

Pablo Coto-Millán
Utility and Production
1999. 3-7908-1153-X

Frank Riedel
Imperfect Information and Investor Heterogeneity in the Bond Market
2000. ISBN 3-7908-1247-1

Kirsten Ralf
Business Cycles
2000. ISBN 3-7908-1245-5

Michele Bagella/Leonardo Becchetti (Eds.)
The Competitive Advantage of Industrial Districts
2000. ISBN 3-7908-1254-4

Frank Bohn
Monetary Union and Fiscal Stability
2000. ISBN 3-7908-1266-8

Michael Malakellis
Integrated Macro-Micro-Modelling Under Rational Expectations
2000. ISBN 3-7908-1274-9

Jaime Behar

Cooperation and Competition in a Common Market

Studies on the Formation of MERCOSUR

With 9 Figures
and 60 Tables

Springer-Verlag Berlin Heidelberg GmbH

Series Editors
Werner A. Müller
Martina Bihn

Author
Ass. Prof. Jaime Behar
Institute of Latin American Studies
University of Stockholm
10691 Stockholm
Sweden

ISSN 1431-1933
ISBN 978-3-7908-1280-0

Cataloging-in-Publication Data applied for
Die Deutsche Bibliothek – CIP-Einheitsaufnahme
Behar, Jaime: Cooperation and competition in a common market: studies on the formation of MERCOSUR; with 60 tables / Jaime Behar. – Heidelberg: Physica-Verl., 2000
(Contributions to economics)

ISBN 978-3-7908-1280-0 ISBN 978-3-642-57650-8 (eBook)
DOI 10.1007/978-3-642-57650-8

Originally published by Physica-Verlag Heidelberg New York in 2000

Softcover-Design: Erich Kirchner, Heidelberg

SPIN 10756483 88/2202-5 4 3 2 1 0 – Printed on acid-free paper

Preface

The essays included in this book are the result of seven years of research spanning the 1990-1997 period. Most of them have been published in scientific magazines or as chapters of books. To the end of this edition, and in order to avoid repetitions, the original texts have been modified, particularly with regard to the titles and introductions of the chapters.

Chapter two reproduces the article "Economic Integration and Intra-Industry Trade: The Case of the Argentine-Brazilian Free Trade Agreement", published in the *Journal of Common Markets* (vol XXIX, No 5, pp. 527-552, sept. 1991). Chapter three originates from an empirical study prepared for UNIDO, the United Nations Industrial Development Organization. The analytical framework and the preliminary conclusions of that work appeared in a working paper "The MERCOSUR Pattern of Intra-Industry Trade" (RP No 75, Stockholm: LAIS, 1997). Chapter four was published with the title "Plant-size Effects of Trade: The Case of MERCOSUR Countries" as a chapter of the book *Growth Trade and Integration in Latin America* (W. Karlsson and A. Malaki (eds.), Stockholm: LAIS, pp. 297-319, 1996). Chapter five in turn corresponds to the article entitled "Measuring the Effects of Economic Integration for the Southern Cone Countries: Industry Simulations of Trade Liberalization" as published in *The Developing Economies* (Vol. XXXIII, No 1, pp. 1-31, mars 1995). Finally, chapter six is the revised and updated version of the paper presented at the First European Congress of Latinamericanists, which took place at Salamanca, Spain in June 1996.

Preliminary versions of the chapters were submitted for academic inquiry on different occasions. In this preface, I would like to express my gratitude to the participants of the seminaries organized by the Swedish Institute for Social Research and the Institute of Latin American Studies, both at the Stockholm University; the Stockholm School of Economics; and the Department of Economics, Universidad de la República, Montevideo. Thanks are also due to the participants in the workshop "Regional Economic Integration" organized by the University of Salamanca.

During the process of recollecting and processing the data, I received the support of numerous colleagues and the cooperation of many officials working at national and international agencies to whom I express my gratitude. Among them, I would specially like to mention G. Gual, University of Navarra; L. Torres, Autonomous University of Barcelona; I. Terra, M. Vaillant and M. Stein, Universidad de la República, Montevideo; G. R. Gigena and R. Oliveira at the central office of LAIA, Montevideo; R. Grosskoff and M. D. Fernández at DGEC, and W. Alpuin at DGCE, Montevideo; L. Botti at INDEG and M. Blanco at Central Bank, Buenos Aires; N. de Castro Senra and S. Bezerra, at IBGE, Rio de Janeiro; and F. Sercovich at UNIDO, Vienna.

Financial support for the research was provided by the Department for Research Cooperation of Sida, the Swedish International Cooperation Agency.

November 1999

Jaime Behar
Institute of Latin American Studies
Stockholm University

Contents

1 Introduction ---------- **1**

2 Industrial Adjustment, Product Differentiation and Economies of Scale ---------- **9**

2.1 Objectives and Provisions of the PICEAB ---------- 9
2.2 Economic Integration and the Gains from Intra-Industry Trade ---------- 11
2.2.1 Industrial Adjustment. ---------- 12
2.2.2 Product Differentiation ---------- 12
2.2.3 Economies of Scale ---------- 14
2.3 Empirical Analysis ---------- 15
2.3.1 The Extent of Inter-Industry Adjustments ---------- 15
2.3.2 Product Differentiation and Intra-Industry Specialization ---------- 17
2.3.3 Economies of Scale ---------- 24
2.4 Concluding Remarks ---------- 27

3 Patterns of Intra-Industry Trade ---------- **29**

3.1 Evolution of Intra-MERCOSUR Trade ---------- 30
3.2 Measurement Problems ---------- 34
3.3 The Extent of MERCOSUR Intra-Industry Trade ---------- 35
3.4 Analysis by Product Group ---------- 38
3.5 Vertical Differentiation *versus* Horizontal Differentiation ---------- 42
3.6 The Impact of Regional Integration ---------- 45
3.7 Conclusions ---------- 49

4 Plant-Size Effects of Trade ---------- **51**

4.1 Differences in Plant Size ---------- 51
4.2 Factors Determining Production Scale ---------- 53
4.3 The Rationale of the Variables Included in the Model ---------- 55
4.3.1 Trade Variables ---------- 55
4.3.2 Cost and Market Size ---------- 57
4.3.3 Market Concentration and Labor Productivity ---------- 57
4.4 Data Sources and Model Specification ---------- 57
4.5 Empirical Issues and Regression Results ---------- 59
4.5.1 Product Lines ---------- 59

4.5.2 Industry Level ---------- 60
4.6 Analysis of Results ---------- 65
4.7 Concluding Remarks ---------- 67

5 Cooperation and Competition
Industry Simulations of Trade Liberalization ---------- 69
5.1 Description of the Model and the Calibration Procedure ---------- 69
5.1.1 The Model ---------- 70
5.1.2 Calibration ---------- 71
5.2 Sources of Data and Exogenous Parameters ---------- 75
5.3 Simulating Trade Liberalization ---------- 77
5.3.1 Reducing Trade Barriers ---------- 79
5.3.2 Welfare Gains ---------- 79
5.3.3 Changes in Output and Average Costs ---------- 84
5.3.4 Bertrand *versus* Cournot ---------- 88
5.4 Customs Union and Foreign Exchange Policy ---------- 89
5.4.1 The Effects of a Common Tariff ---------- 95
5.4.2 The Effects of Disparities in Exchange Rate ---------- 96
5.5 Concluding Remarks ---------- 96

6 Economic Integration and Economic Divergence ---------- 103
6.1 Overall Trade Liberalization as a New Integration Framework ---------- 103
6.2 Increased Economic Interdependence ---------- 105
6.3 Disparities in Monetary Conditions and Stabilization Measures ---------- 108
6.3.1 Inflation Rates ---------- 109
6.3.2 Exchange Rates ---------- 110
6.3.3 Stabilization Policies ---------- 111
6.4 Divergences in Economic Performance ---------- 114
6.4.1 Income Disparities ---------- 114
6.4.2 Rates of Growth ---------- 115
6.4.3 External Performance ---------- 116
6.5. Concluding Remarks ---------- 118

Methodological Appendix ---------- 121

Statistical Appendix ---------- 125

References ---------- 147

Index ---------- 151

1 Introduction

The studies collected in this book were written at different times and for varying purposes. However, each one, in its own way, is intended to shed light on a single issue, namely the economic rationale of the Southern Common Market (MERCOSUR [Mercado Común del Sur]). This is not an easy task since the reasons for the failure of Latin American integration attempts in the past are still not well understood and even less the dynamics of current processes. The case of LAFTA (Latin American Free Trade Association) – the largest and most ambitious integration program in the sixties and the seventies – is illustrative of the issue. Neither the long-term objective of completely eliminating trade barriers among the member countries, nor the more modest one of progressively widening the common list of tariff-free commodities was achieved. Today, different analysts agree that the failure of LAFTA was related to the misconception of economic integration among developing countries as embodied in the LAFTA agreement, namely its excessive emphasis on discriminatory practices and the elaboration of complex rules for promoting intra-regional trade. Other authors, however, contend that the main problem was the absence of mechanisms that could guarantee a more equal distribution of the gains and costs from regional trade liberalization.

The stagnation of trade negotiations within the LAFTA led to the reorganization of the latter into a more flexible scheme, the LAIA (Latin American Integration Association), in 1980. The LAIA agreement continued recognizing multilateral negotiation as the main instrument for achieving reductions in tariffs on intra-regional trade on a global basis (the regional preferential tariff). In practice, however, LAIA has evolved to be an institutional framework for the liberalization of tariff barriers among members on a bilateral basis. In other words, two or more countries can negotiate larger reciprocal tariff cuts without this implying any obligation to grant a similar preference to other countries. Paradoxically, this has increased the likelihood of achieving a free trade area embracing all of South American countries.

On the one hand, the proliferation of bilateral trade agreements has accentuated the trend towards the fragmentation of the region, a problem that LAFTA had failed to solve in the past. But, on the other hand, there is no doubt that LAIA has been effective, particularly in what relates to the growth of intraregional trade and the encouragement of economic cooperation in other areas. The main reason for this is that by allowing the countries to associate freely according to geographical proximity, cultural affinity or weaker disparities in levels of development, LAIA has diminished the risk for collisions of national interests. It has facilitated the achievement of durable trade agreements and, ultimately, strengthened the attractiveness of economic integration for the more reluctant countries.

The accuracy of these assertions was confirmed in 1988 when Argentina and Brazil, the two largest and most industrialized South American countries, agreed to accelerate the process of bilateral trade liberalization. The advancements in economic integration made by these two countries in subsequent years, as well as the importance they have for the entire region, compelled Uruguay and Paraguay as well as Bolivia and Chile to join the Argentine-Brazilian trade agreement; the two first countries as full members and the other two as associates. A new cooperation treaty, the Treaty of Asuncion, was signed by Argentina, Brazil, Paraguay and Uruguay in March 1991, and the time schedule for achieving tariff-free trade established by Brazil and Argentina was maintained. At the same time, the countries committed themselves to initiating a process of tariff alignment. The objective was to converge toward a low common external tariff (CET) as compared with members' pre-union tariffs. In August 1994, the presidents of the four countries agreed to establish a (imperfect) customs union by January 1, 1995.[1]

By 1996, MERCOSUR comprised nearly 206 million people, who generated a GDP of $664 billion (in 1990 prices). In the same year MERCOSUR's industrial production was 60 per cent of LAIA's. This makes MERCOSUR the second largest trading block in the Western Hemisphere[2] and the most promising attempt at integration in Latin America as the rapid growth in trade within the group illustrates. In 1991, intra-MERCOSUR exports amounted to $5.2 billion and represented 14 per cent of total exports. Corresponding values for 1997 were $20.3 billion and 25 per cent.

A New Rationale for Latin American Integration

In its diverse modalities, preferential trade agreements, free-trade areas, customs unions, etc., regional integration appears to be the outcome of the interaction of a variety of factors that merge in a rather complex fashion and can hardly be explained in strict economic terms. Conversely, it can be verified that, when successful, economic integration produces changes across the societies involved, the nature of which is not only economic, but social and political as well. This is

---

[1] In practice, this means the elimination of tariff and non-tariff barriers on trade among member countries and a CET between zero and 20 per cent for third-country imports with some exceptions. MERCOSUR countries are allowed a list of 1,019 products on which they can set their own external tariffs. Out of these, 300 are included in Argentina's and Brazil's lists.

[2] After the North American Free Trade Area (NAFTA) which comprises Canada, Mexico, and the United States.

not to suggest that deriving arguments for or against integration from analysis of economic data is an exercise in futility. Quite the contrary, the relevant literature gives account of the impressive amount of empirical work that has been devoted to drawing conclusions from economic phenomena attributable to regional integration and the notable efforts made to consistently incorporate these conclusions into a modern theory of trade and integration. More often than not, the results of such efforts, coupled with the criteria embodied in said theory, have had a decisive influence on policy makers when shaping and implementing integration agreements. It must be recognized, however, that whatever the sophistication of the methods used or the reliability of the data analyzed, such criteria and recommendations constitute only one of the many elements for judging the motives and factors impelling specific integration processes.

Even in the area of economic studies, it is difficult to make general statements about the rationale of integration. Consider, for instance, analyses of European integration in the sixties and the seventies. A major part of these studies posed the question of the rationale of integration in the terms of the effects of the harmonization of member states' trade policies on allocative efficiency and economic growth, while neglecting the obstacles to integration arising from divergencies in monetary and exchange policies. These provided a motive for concern but certainly not a major one since, in the occurrence of external shocks, which could jeopardize the liberalization of intra-regional trade, the countries were able to cooperate in achieving monetary stabilization. When analyzing the reasons for the rapid advancements in economic integration made by Latin American countries in recent years, a similar approach could be adopted. The fact is, however, that the economic political conditions surrounding these attempts highly diverge from those prevailing in Europe in past decades. Certainly, macroeconomic instability has been endemic in Latin America with the result that each and every attempt at integration has been fraught with uncertainty from the very outset. The relevant literature, including this book, provide numerous references to the dilution of such initiatives, owing to the failure of member countries to stabilize their exchange markets, attain balance-of-payments equilibrium, reduce inflation rates and avoid the debt trap. Even if the source and shape of such failures differ according to the country and period examined, there is no doubt that inconsistent domestic policy and the lack of coordination in the efforts to achieve macroeconomic equilibrium have been major factors in undermining integration efforts.

A new approach to the rationale of current efforts to integration in Latin America seems to emerge from this context; namely that of making domestic decisions irrevocable and consistent with common stabilization objectives. This approach is used throughout this book, in an effort to qualify the conclusions of the analysis of specific integration issues. It is also the basis of the analysis in *Chapter 6*. This chapter focuses on the benefits of promoting policy coordination in a framework of growing economic interdependence and divergence among the South American countries.

COOPERATION *VERSUS* COMPETITION

Some fifteen years ago, I compared the European and Latin American experiences in integration and concluded that what the two had in common, if anything, was the fact that they were driven by market forces, and, therefore, by two apparently contradictory principles, namely cooperation and competition (Behar, 1980). The political drift toward integration in both Europe and Latin America, I posited, could conceivably be crystallized in a diversity of economic cooperation agreements, which turned out to be the case. But, in both regions, the terms of cooperation were invariably the outcome of asymmetric power relations, continuously eroded by the competition engine propelling the entire process.

The history of Latin American integration provides some illustrative examples of these contradictory developments. In the case of South American countries, for instance, the same economic and political transformation that made obsolete the isolationist and autarkic ideas prevailing in the forties and the fifties paved the way for the open regionalism of the present decade. This was, however a long and arduous road, deviating repeatedly from the ideal of cooperation among neighbors for fear of unequal competition capacity. As early as 1953, a project proposing the integration of Argentina, Brazil, Chile and Uruguay was presented at a meeting of the Economic Commission for Latin America (ECLA), but failed to gain approval. It would take forty years for an operative common market agreement to be reached which would ultimately include the foregoing countries and Paraguay. In the meantime, the countries of South America continued to develop separately, protecting their economies from competition both from outside the region and from neighbors. Even if the political and intellectual expectations surrounding the integration process remained unchanged in subsequent decades, the fact is that integration continued to be looked upon as the extension of protectionist policies to the regional level, and these same policies were viewed as the true way to economic development.

The shift from import substitution policies and strong government intervention to economic liberalization and privatization of state-owned enterprises, as accomplished in the eighties, has called for a re-thinking of the motives for integration. On the one hand, the working assumptions of ECLA theorists, as formulated at the end of World War II, that liberalization may lead to deindustrialization, have been confirmed, in part. Certainly, stronger competition from abroad has revealed the fragility and vulnerability of the Latin American economies. In the case of MERCOSUR, small-scale, inefficient domestic industries producing consumer goods are being seriously damaged by the major influx of less expensive foreign substitutes, while large-scale industries producing intermediate goods, capital equipment or major consumer durables are seeing their market position considerably weaken *vis-à-vis* foreign competitors. These large-scale industries currently face growing difficulties in their efforts to modernize, due to a combination of increased investment costs and elimination of direct or indirect subventions.

On the other hand, however, trade has expanded rapidly, with intra-group trade accounting for most of that growth and new all-time records being reached continuously. This has made two important facts very clear to policy makers and firms. First, maximization of the gains of associating with neighbors now depends on the establishment of fair rules for competition in the prospective common market rather than on the negotiation of mutual restrictions on competition in the local markets, as was the case in the past. Second, cooperation agreements should be inspired by and serve nothing but this purpose. In this context, the regional *versus* overall trade liberalization controversy that drew so much of the attention, if not the time and energy, of researchers and policy makers in the eighties lost most of its relevance. As the economic reform program advances and the alignment of domestic prices with world prices improves, other factors affecting competitiveness which had been neglected heretofore are now being addressed, such as geographical proximity, similarities in consumption patterns and scale of production. Certainly, with trade barriers weakening considerably, trade policies tending to converge, and tariff-spread significantly contracting, the differential impact of the above mentioned factors on production costs and, consequently, their importance for competition truly increase. The impressive volume of infrastructure projects currently being implemented or in the planning stage, coupled with the recent notable growth of mergers, joint ventures and mutual direct investment, speak for the importance attached to said differential impacts by Southern Cone governments and firms. In the short term, these phenomena should encourage large-scale investments by both local and foreign firms. This evidently could enhance productivity and promote product specialization, but may also reinforce the trend toward market concentration and the diffusion of imperfect forms of competition.

In conclusion, instead of inward-looking policies based on defensive cooperation, or outward-looking policies based on countries quiescently adapting to the prescriptions of orthodox trade theory, the current integration process of Southern Cone countries heralds inward-outward developments through offensive competition on both the regional and the world markets. *Chapter 5* of this book focuses on these issues, using a partial equilibrium model that incorporates economies of scale and differentiated products.

Trade as a Source of Scale Efficiency

It has been widely recognized that the liberalization of trade is one of the main sources of economic growth for the individual country. A more controversial question is whether trade is always a source of economic efficiency. On the one hand, it should be recognized that if one assumes that perfect competition and constant returns to scale prevail in export markets, the answer is clearly yes. Undoubtedly, under these conditions, economic theory shows that the complete openness of the national economy removes distortions to the allocation of resources between domestic and world market-oriented activities, encouraging a rationalization of these activities and eradicating inefficient business practices. And this is the case whether or not the other countries are headed in the same direction.

In practice, however, the original question becomes more complex since real conditions on the world market for products clearly diverge from those corresponding to the simplified environment described above. Consider for instance the conditions of competition. As a matter of fact, the effects of general trade liberalization or reciprocal tariff reductions on economic efficiency depend on the strategic reactions of local firms to both growing competition from abroad on the home market and to enhanced access to partners' markets. Nonetheless, if this does not happen in an essentially non-cooperative framework, then, to predict the direction and nature of these reactions becomes a much more difficult task. With interactions between a few firms dominating competition and allowing for collusion, it is fitting to ask whether the effect of an increase in competition on efficiency will be evenly distributed. Consider, for instance, those industries already benefiting from cost advantages in the form of increasing returns. In this case, the likelihood for firms having a non-competitive perception of their domestic market increases. As a consequence, increased import exposure will not necessarily stimulate firms to search for scale-based cost efficiency. It can further lead to the displacement of those firms that were producing at clearly sub-optimal levels because of both the limited dimensions of domestic demand and high protection levels. Easier access to foreign markets can, however, have a number of positive effects on size-related cost efficiency. The prospects of increased exports can indeed raise the level of capacity-utilization at the plant level, making it possible to reap additional benefits from unexploited economies of scale. It can further encourage existing firms to large-scale investments. These issues are approached empirically in *Chapter 4* by means of an econometric model of the determinants of plant size. The estimation of the model is conducted in both physical and value terms. Its results provide an indicator of the extent to which trade flows influence MERCOSUR firms' decisions to increase or reduce plant size.

INTRA-INDUSTRY TRADE AND BEYOND

If economies of scale and imperfect competition are important issues to the dynamics of MERCOSUR, the effects of trade liberalization on member countries' specialization pattern should necessarily differ from those predicted by classical customs union theory. More specifically, the actual pattern of trade that would emerge would be more of the intra-industry than of the inter-industry type. In addition, the existence of such factors as similar demand conditions, geographical proximity and implementation by the countries of similar economic reform programs should reinforce this trend and make it apparent even at the pre-integration stage. *Chapters 2* and *3* are devoted to analysis of these issues.

The framework for *Chapter 2* is the Argentine-Brazilian Free Trade Agreement that predated MERCOSUR by five years. Accordingly, the analysis focuses on the costs and benefits of the liberalization of bilateral trade in terms of inter-industry adjustment, intra-industry specialization, and economies of scale in these two countries. The results advance some of the conclusions that are drawn in *Chapter 5* and point, in particular, to the stronger competitive position and the higher technological level of Brazilian firms *vis-à-vis* Argentine firms, as well as the former's greater ability to draw economies-of-scale gains from integration. *Chapter 3* considers changes in the pattern of intra-MERCOSUR trade in manufactures during the 1975-1990 pre-integration period, and provides a detailed inventory of these changes in relation to both the direction of trade flows and the nature of the goods exchanged. Intra-industry trade indices are computed for different sub-periods, and diverse hypotheses about the factors behind that trade are examined and tested, namely technological innovation and trade in vertically differentiated products.

2 Industrial Adjustment, Product Differentiation and Economies of Scale

In July 1986, the governments of Argentina and Brazil announced the institution of a broad program of economic cooperation between the two countries (PICEAB [Programa de Integración y Cooperación Económica Argentina-Brasil]) which stipulated, among other objectives, the elimination of all barriers to reciprocal trade over a ten-year period. Successive negotiations brought the deadline for achieving zero tariffs on bilateral trade forward by five years. This chapter examines retrospectively the objectives and instruments established by the PICEAB, drawing on the arguments advanced in recent contributions to trade theory. The focus is on three related issues, namely the extent of the industrial adjustment which would follow the full liberalization of Argentine-Brazilian bilateral trade; the pre-integration level of intra-industry trade in manufactures; and the potential gains from product differentiation and economies of scale which would be produced by the PICEAB.

2.1 Objectives and Provisions of the PICEAB

The Statement on Cooperation and Integration formed the basis for the PICEAB. It consisted of a preamble and 12 protocols specifying cooperation objectives in areas such as bilateral trade, basic food production, industrial investment and energy. In subsequent years, another 12 protocols were signed and the Agreement was extended to cover transport, communications and monetary cooperation. Here we shall concentrate on the protocols that provided for the liberalization of reciprocal trade. These are the protocols eliminating barriers to bilateral trade in products from the capital goods sector and the motor car industry, and the protocols establishing mechanisms to reduce tariffs and quotas on the other goods.

As stated in the preamble of the Agreement, the trade liberalization program should aim to produce an overall balanced trade growth, sector by sector. In order to avoid extreme trade imbalances and to allow time for domestic firms to adapt to increased competition, the two countries agreed to phase in the liberalization program over several years. In the capital goods industry, all kinds of custom barriers, both tariff and non-tariff restrictions to bilateral trade in 286 products (the 'common list') were removed when the Agreement came into force at the beginning of 1987. An enlargement of the common list was agreed upon in July 1987, raising the number of liberalized items to 356. Successive rounds of negotiation increased the number of items on the common list until it covered all those included in the annex to protocol 1, that is, about 600 items. In turn, the automotive agreement (protocol 21) which was signed in April 1988 provided for duty-free imports of new cars, but restrained bilateral exports to a maximum of 5,000 units in 1989 and to 10,000 in 1990. Trade in automobile parts was to be regulated by a "common list" as in the case of capital goods. The scheme was completed by protocols 4 and 22. The former incorporated into the PICEAB the partial trade preferences negotiated within the LAIA, and formalized in the Agreement of Partial Scope 1 (APS1), while the latter established the progressive reduction of tariffs on bilateral trade in processed foods. At the time of the signing of the PICEAB, the APS1 covered about 3,000 items. In later years, this number was substantially augmented and the level of mutual tariff reductions increased. In June 1988, 271 items for Argentina and 355 items for Brazil were added to the national lists while the level of tariff reductions was increased by 10 and 5 per cent respectively (INTAL, monthly).

Central features of the PICEAB were the implementation of mechanisms for creating balanced trade expansion and the establishment of rules for safeguard actions. The former included bilateral lines of credit for a maximum of $200 million and the specifying of critical parameters. These parameters defined situations of "dynamic trade balance" on the basis of the ratio of fixed values of the trade deficit to trade volume. Two adjustment mechanisms were implemented in order to keep actual ratios beneath fixed ratios: periodical revisions of the common list of preferences, and the provision of additional financing resources by the countries' Central Banks. Rules for safeguard actions included restoring tariffs or quotas in cases where the elimination of bilateral trade barriers would cause substantial harm to domestic production.

Three additional arrangements concerning the capital goods sector deserve mention. First, the two countries agreed to work for a rapid convergence of their respective external tariff, that is, of their levels of protection with respect to a third country. Second, capital goods produced in one country were to receive national treatment in the other country, provided they were included in the common list. A necessary condition for this was that the degree of national integration (the level of domestic content) was not to be less than 80 per cent. Finally, the public sector of each country was to give firms in the partner country preferential treatment when buying capital goods.

As we see from the description above, the Agreement eliminated all barriers on trade in capital goods, and envisaged the formation of a customs union for this sector in the future, whereas it retained considerable restrictive measures ranging from quotas to tariffs on bilateral trade in other goods. This suggests that a central aim of the Agreement was to promote intra-industry specialization[1] with the

[1] The preamble in fact corroborated this impression. It postulated that "The (PICEAB) must be equilibrated in the sense that it should not promote the specialization of the economies in specific sectors but promote intra-sectoral integration".

capital goods sector playing the role of the pivotal industry. One implication of this is that policy makers in both countries believed that greater benefits would accrue from bilateral trade liberalization if it were implemented with the objective of promoting intra-industry rather than inter-industry trade. Another is that this effect would be stronger and easier to achieve in the capital goods sector. At this juncture the question arises as to which arguments support these presumptions.

2.2 Economic Integration and the Gains from Intra-Industry Trade

Two empirical observations which have received increasing attention in the recent trade literature are the growing importance of intra-industry trade for world trade, and the fact that discriminatory trade arrangements have become the dominant post-war form of commercial policy.

Drawing on the evidence provided by several studies, Greenaway (1989) concludes that there is a causal link between these two phenomena and that this has been corroborated for both developed and developing countries. The same author points out, however, that the theoretical analysis of the underlying mechanisms is still unsatisfactory and that their empirical relevance is strongly related to country-specific assumptions. In other words, intra-industry trade may be stimulated by economic integration, but this effect is mediated by factors such as preference diversity and overlapping demand, decreasing costs in production and intra-firm trade, oligopolistic competition and product differentiation.

Economic integration and intra-industry trade have also been described as two phenomena, occurring independently, which are generated by other basic forces. These forces need be identified and the ways they shape actual trade flows and/or influence the formation of trade blocs explained, but there is no obvious link between the two issues. In earlier studies, arguments in support of this hypothesis were usually based on empirical tests rather than theoretical reasoning (e.g. Pomfret, 1979; Caves, 1981). At present, the analytical separation of intra-industry trade and economic integration is a fact, as can be seen in the large number of studies which alternatively concentrate on one or another of the two issues, disregarding the link.

A third logical alternative – that growing intra-industry trade as an independent phenomenon can provide a motive for economic integration – has usually been ignored in the literature. This presumably depends on the difficulties in finding some rationale for this hypothesis within the framework of trade theory. The notion that the objective of increasing intra-industry trade can push integration forward, however, makes sense when translated into the real world of trade negotiations and conflicts. Drabek and Greenaway (1984) pointed out that customs unions may be formed with the deliberate purpose of promoting inter as opposed to intra-industry trade. As the discussion in the previous section showed, the PICEAB addresses the opposite issue, namely the benefits that countries may draw from basing integration on increased intra-industry specialization.

2.2.1 Industrial Adjustment

Several studies dealing with the costs and benefits of economic integration focus on the rationalization process that trade liberalization brings about. Though no concluding empirical evidence has been provided (cf. Richardson, 1989), a usual view is that the adjustments costs associated with any free trade agreement are likely to be greater when the loss of trade barriers leads to inter-industry instead of intra-industry specialization (e.g. Wonnacott, 1987). One argument supporting this is that the former type of specialization may well be efficient in the long run, but it necessarily produces serious dislocation in both production and employment in the short run. Conversely, intra-industry specialization would make the adjustment process less disruptive. First, it would be easier for firms and plants to cease producing a given line of goods and to start producing a closely defined variety, than to move to another type of industry. Second, changes in income distribution arising from trade liberalization would not be so dramatic under conditions of intra-industry specialization. Krugman (1981), for example, uses a simplified two-economy, two-industry, two-factor model to show that both productive factors gain from trade when it takes the intra-industry form. His analysis, which incorporates economies of scale and monopolistic competition, suggests that on the whole distribution problems arising from trade in differentiated products are not so serious as those associated with inter-industry trade. This has recently been corroborated by Norman (1990) who used a family of models calibrated to actual EC and EFTA data for comparing the welfare effects of tariff reductions under alternative market conditions.

2.2.2 Product Differentiation

Two of the most common assumptions made in models of intra-industry trade are, first, that this type of trade is associated with imperfectly competitive product markets and, second, that the output of relevant industries consists of sufficiently differentiated products.[2] Both assumptions have important implications for the analysis of the gains from trade and trade policy.

If intra-industry trade is assumed to be caused by monopolistic competition and product differentiation, and the domestic industry in the two countries is not able to produce all potential varieties, theoretical analysis shows that the number of available products will probably be larger after the two (closed) economies begin trading with each other (Krugman, 1990; Venables, 1987a). In such

[2] Models of intra-industry trade based on alternative assumptions are, for instance: Falvey and Kierzkowsky's (1987) perfect competition model and Brander's (1981) model of intra-industry trade in identical commodities.

circumstances, consumers in both countries would get additional gains from bilateral trade in the form of wider product variety, provided that this is assumed to have a value in its own right.

The situation described above is that of two autarkical economies which open reciprocal trade. A question that follows naturally relates to the effects of tariff intervention in the presence of trade; more specifically, whether a tariff reduction unambiguously leads to increased product variety in the case of two trading economies.[3] In their study of commercial policy under imperfect competition, Greenaway and Milner (1986) answered this question in the affirmative, arguing that even in this case protection "simply reverts the effect of the opening of free trade". In fact, Falvey (1981) had already proved this by using a model where product differentiation was defined as differences in quality, and demand for each quality was taken to be a function of the prices of all qualities.

Changes in the specification of the utility function may modify this conclusion, however. Helpman and Krugman (1989), for example, showed that when product differentiation is associated with product variety, and all varieties enter symmetrically into demand, an *ad valorem* tariff does not affect the number of goods produced in each country. Richardson (1989) in turn cited the case where consumers' preferences are governed by brand image associated with "foreign status" (pseudo-differentiation). Under these circumstances, trade liberalization may shift a country's demand for a given domestically produced good towards a closer but imperfect substitute produced abroad by some prestigious firm. This may provoke the exit of domestic firms and ultimately result in a reduction of product variety. More generally Venables (1987b) used a model of (Chamberlinian) monopolistic competition to show that, under the assumption of no retaliation, the imposition of a (small) tariff by one of two trading economies may increase the total number of product types available.

An alternative model of intra-industry trade based on neo-Hotelling monopolistic competition and economies of scales, which allows for tariff manipulation, is provided in Lancaster (1984). This author introduces the hypothesis of asymmetrical preferences to differentiated products, and proves that under these circumstances free trade does raise product variety when it is compared with autarky. However, when the reference situation is restricted trade instead, because of a non-prohibitive tariff, Lancaster's model leads us to the opposite conclusion, that is, that the complete liberalization of trade may reduce product variety and therefore produce welfare losses.

Finally, it should be added that even when competition is modeled to be of the oligopolistic instead of the more monopolistic type, the outcome of opening trade as regards product variety remains uncertain. An example of this is provided by

[3] Note that we are not concerned here with the impact of trade liberalization on intra-industry trade as such but on intra-industry specialization. See Greenway and Milner (1986) for a detailed assessment of the differences between both concepts.

Eaton and Kierzkowsky's model (1984), where the effects on product variety depend on the number of producers in each country.

It is worth noting here that the diversity of results produced by the analytical approaches just described stresses the need for more theoretical research on the role of economies of scale and imperfect competition in trade. But, as stated by Helpman and Krugman (1989), "it is better to have a collection of examples that seem to capture what is actually going on than to restrict oneself to a fully integrated theory that does not".

A common feature of the theoretical approaches to product differentiation mentioned above is that they draw on assumptions about consumer behavior. Accordingly, the conclusions would apply to consumer goods exclusively. Intermediate and capital goods, however, constitute a large share of world trade, and do record significant indices of intra-industry trade. A few authors, such as Ethier (1979 and 1982) and Kol and Rayment (1989), have made statements to this effect for the case of intermediate goods. They approach the question in terms of vertical specialization, meaning that the exchange of similar intermediate goods in fact reflects outward processing rather than horizontal (or vertical) product differentiation. Similar explanations could also apply to the exchange of final products (consumer or capital goods) for its components. According to this approach, welfare gains from intra-industry trade and product differentiation in intermediate goods would mainly be associated with gains in efficiency, emanating from vertical specialization.

Models of product differentiation and intra-industry specialization adapted to the conditions of the capital goods sector are even more rare. One of the few authors who have devoted attention to this question is Jacobsson (1988). His econometric test of the determinants of intra-industry specialization in the Swedish capital goods sector is in line with Rosenberg's (1976) hypothesis about the importance of dynamic economies of scales in that sector. In Jacobson's study, dynamic economies of scale are defined in terms of larger technical efforts and a greater number of specialized sub-industries within a given statistically defined industry. In this case, product variety is thus defined in terms of technological rather than horizontal differentiation, and the driving factor is R & D rather than consumer's preferences. Product improvement and increased division of labor among firms, as well as raising productivity and lower resource cost in purchasing industries, would be the gains from increased supply of variety within the capital goods sector (Richardson, 1989).

2.2.3 Economies of Scale

Economies of scale are another source of gains from intra-industry trade based on product differentiation. As showed by Falvey (1981) and Falvey and Kierzkowsky (1987), product differentiation can be consistent with the assumption of constant returns to scale provided that the former is defined in terms of product quality (meaning product improvement or deterioration) and according to some specific production conditions (vertical product differentiation). Most authors, however, take the view that product differentiation depends mainly on slight differences in product characteristics, which are still relevant for the formation of consumers' preferences (horizontal product differentiation). This approach leads immediately to the hypothesis of increasing returns. The assumption is necessary in order to explain why the number of products produced in one industry fall short of the number of potentially differentiated products, though demand is providing continual incentive for firms to increase product variety (cf. Eaton and Lipsey, 1989). In this framework, the countries would gain from trade liberalization because this stimulates intra-industry trade, thus raising the number of products available in home markets. Trade liberalization would also create conditions for achieving minimum efficient scale in the new production lines, or reaping unexploited product-specific economies of scale in existing industries. Alternatively, gains in the form of economies of scope would eventually be produced if the post-trade increase in product variety were due instead to an increase in the number of production processes observed in individual firms.

2.3 Empirical Analysis

2.3.1 The Extent of Inter-Industry Adjustments

A first approximation of the potential inter-industry adjustment that would follow a comprehensive and hypothetical free trade agreement between Argentina and Brazil is shown in Table 2.1. The numbers in the sixth column of the table are Argentina's net exports to Brazil expressed as percentages of total bilateral trade. They may be regarded as indicators of the (revealed) comparative advantages of one of the two countries with respect to the other. Clearly, this interpretation is open to objection on the ground that the ratios will be influenced by tariffs on imports from third country and by non-tariff barriers on trade between partners. We must therefore emphasize that the approach here only allows for tentative conclusions. With this approach, commodities having a positive sign in column 6 would be those in which Argentina has comparative advantage with respect to Brazil. Only four such cases can be pinpointed in the table, all of them agricultural products with a low degree of processing. Note that two other natural resource-based industries, namely the food and the mineral products industries get a negative indicator but the order of magnitude is very low. In the remaining cases Brazil appears to have a strong comparative advantage when trading with Argentina.

According to this analysis, a bilateral agreement that eliminates trade barriers on all products would induce significant short-term pressures on most Argentine manufacturing industries. This would be particularly true in the cases where the nominal tariff faced by Brazilian exporters is relatively high and Brazil's

Table 2.1. Comparative advantages and nominal tariffs in Argentine-Brazilian trade. Millions of current dollars and percentages

Sections of BTN	Tariff Brazil (1)	Tariff Argentina (2)	Tariff Diff. (3)	Imports from partner Brazil (4)	Imports from partner Argentina (5)	Imports from partner Ratio (6)
Live animals; animal products	3	3	0	6362	3562	28.21
Vegetable products	3	0	-3	131148	40023	53.24
Fats and oils	5	3	-2	40847	1139	94.57
Food, beverages and tobacco	27	3	-24	17191	18283	-3.08
Mineral products	4	7	3	51380	75190	-18.81
Chemical and allied industries	7	11	4	31266	116628	-57.72
Artificial resins, plastic, rubber	18	31	13	5582	58841	-82.67
Raw hides and skins, leather, etc.	9	15	6	41414	45	99.78
Wood and wood articles	9	5	-4	0	9344	-100.00
Paper and paperboard	7	4	-3	905	26544	-93.41
Textiles and textile articles	6	5	-1	325	33140	-98.06
Footwear, headgear, etc.	5	11	6	0	95	-100.00
Articles of stone, glass, etc.	7	10	3	1191	7048	-71.09
Pearls, precious metals, etc.	10	12	2	0	62	-100.00
Base metals	16	1	-15	3523	89616	-92.43
Machinery and electrical equip.	15	6	-9	13701	98315	-75.54
Vehicles and parts	23	17	-6	11667	66762	-70.25
Optical, sound recorders, etc.	13	19	6	720	7776	-83.05
Arms and ammunition	0	0	0	0	678	-100.00
Miscellaneous articles	3	30	27	36	1520	-95.37
Work of art, antiques, etc.	0	0	0	0	0	--

Explanation of columns: (1) 1979 weighted average tariff rates applied to imports from ALADI countries. (2) 1983 weighted average tariff rates applied to imports from ALADI countries. (3) (2)–(1). (4) 1983 Brazilian imports from Argentina. (5) 1983 Argentine imports from Brazil. (6) 100[(4)–(5)] / [(4)+(5)]
Source: Berlinsky et al. (1984) and BID-INTAL (1985)

comparative advantage strongest. Examples of these are artificial resins, plastics and rubber, vehicles and parts, and optical, photographic, etc. An intermediate case, which is still important because of its share in total trade, is the chemical and allied industries. For Brazil, most of the adjustment within the manufacturing sector would be centered on the food industry. As the table shows, the trade balance for the food industry is closer to equilibrium, but the Brazilian level of protection in nominal terms is nine times higher than the Argentine. Short-term impacts are also likely to be produced in those industries for which both the net export ratio and the tariff differential are large and negative. In such cases, as for instance in the base metal industry, the reciprocal elimination of tariffs may produce a considerable increase in Brazilian imports without a corresponding growth in exports.

Our conclusion is that the dismantling of all tariff-barriers to trade between Argentina and Brazil would eventually require considerable inter-industry adjustment in the two countries, but that this adjustment would be more painful for Argentina. Hence it would lie in the interest of the two governments, particularly the Argentine, to negotiate trade liberalization on a more restrictive basis with the intention of seeing to it that most of the overall adjustment would be of the less detrimental intra-industry type.

2.3.2 Product Differentiation and Intra-Industry Specialization

In the previous section, we showed that product differentiation as reflected in trade statistics is liable to diverse interpretations, depending on the type of goods considered. In accordance with this, analysis of intra-industry trade between Argentina and Brazil in this section will be performed separately for consumer, intermediate, and capital goods.[4] As is customary in studies of this type, only the exchange of manufactures (SITC 5 to 8) will be considered.

Table 2.2 provides indices of intra-industry trade by the above-mentioned economic categories for 1986. The indices have been computed in accordance with the methodology stated by Grubel and Lloyd (1975) and Aquino (1978).[5] Indices of intra-industry trade for the years before 1986 as computed in other studies are also displayed in the table. Three main observations can be made: (1) trade between Argentina and Brazil concentrated highly on intermediate goods; (2) the index of intra-industry trade is higher for consumer goods than for the other goods; and (3) there is a tendency towards diminishing intra-industry trade between both countries.

Table 2.2. Argentina-Brazil intra-industry trade indices by broad economic category, 1985

	Manufacturing		Consumer	Intermediate	Capital
Year	Q[a]	GL	Q[a]	Q[a]	Q[a]
1980	44				
1981		35			
1982		29			45
1983		21			
1984		21			
1985		35			
1986	31	29	45	30	35[b]
% share in total trade	100		3	82	15

Q, Aquino-adjusted index; GL, Grubel and Lloyd-unadjusted index

[a] Adjusted for trade imbalance in capital goods

[b] Adjusted for trade imbalance in manufacturing products

Source: Erzan and Laird (1984); Lerda as quoted by Baumann (1989) and own estimations on COMTRADE data

[4] According to the classification stated by the Statistical Office of the United Nations (UN, 1986).

[5] For a discussion on the indices see *Chapter 3*.

Erzan and Laird's (1984) estimate of the Aquino-adjusted index of intra-industry trade (Q) for manufacturing was 44 for the year 1980 while Lerda's (quoted in Baumann, 1989) estimate of the Grubel and Lloyd unadjusted index (GL) was 35 for both 1981 and 1985. These estimates may be compared to our own for 1986 where Q=31 and GL=29. In turn, Chudnovsky's (1985) estimate of intra-industry trade (Q) for capital goods was 45 for 1982, while our own estimation produced an index of 35 for 1986.

2.3.2.1 Consumer Goods

As noted before, analysis of the effects of trade liberalization on product variety in a setting of intra-industry trade leads to diverse and often contradictory results. Product variety can indeed remain constant, increase, or decrease, depending on the modeling of demand side and market structure. Hence, though trade liberalization is likely to stimulate intra-industry trade, there is nothing that guarantees that it would lead to increased diversification in production. Nevertheless, it seems reasonable to expect that the lower the initial level of intra-industry trade in one industry, the more likely it is that trade liberalization will lead to increased intra-industry specialization and thereby to an increase in the number of available product types in that industry.[6] Here we must assume that reciprocal cuts in tariffs and quotas in the framework of the PICEAB will not occur in a symmetrical way as in fact is the case. Otherwise, a partial or total dismantlement of barriers to bilateral trade would most certainly increase the *amount* of intra-industry trade but not necessarily the *proportion* of that trade (cf. Caves, 1981). With these considerations in mind, we turn now to the comparison of levels of intra-industry trade in consumer goods by industry (SITC 3).

Thirty-five of the SITC three-digit items of manufactured products were classified as consumer goods. Of these, 11 were eliminated because of zero values in both exports and imports. Of the remaining items, only those observations with a total value of bilateral trade flows of more than $150,000 or 1 per cent of total trade in consumer goods were retained for analysis. This reduced the sample of industries to the 11 observations displayed in Table 2.3.

When the industries are analyzed one by one, Brazil shows itself as a next exporter in each of the 24 industries recording transactions. Moreover, Argentina's exports were practically nonexistent in five of the 11 sampled industries. It may thus be concluded that the scope for increased intra-industry trade in consumer goods is strongly dependent on future Argentine penetration into Brazilian markets. Note that this conclusion in principle would only apply to those industries showing a low intra-industry index in the table (less than 40 per cent).

Analysis at a less aggregate level, however, indicates that two of the four industries showing high intra-industry trade indices turn out to be representative

[6] This is not to say that bilateral trade liberalization will necessarily eliminate all the cases of (pre-integration) complete inter-industry specialization.

Table 2.3. Argentina-Brazil intra-industry trade indices, 1985. Selected consumer goods

SITC	Description	Share[a]	GL
554	Soap, cleansing, etc.	15	9.60
658	Textile articles n.e.s.	2	0.00
696	Cutlery	8	0.00
775	Household type equip n.e.s.	33	95.17
881	Phot apparatus, equipt n.e.s.	5	48.89
892	Printed matter	6	62.87
893	Articles of plastic n.e.s.	5	41.68
894	Toys, sporting goods, etc.	5	14.08
895	Office supplies n.e.s.	3	25.06
898	Musical instruments n.e.s.	3	0.00
899	Other manufactured goods	13	0.00
All sampled		98	

[a] Percentage of trade in consumer goods
Source: Own estimations based on COMTRADE data

cases of nearly complete inter-industry specialization at the four-digit level. It can indeed be observed in Table 2.4 that Argentina's exports to Brazil are zero or insignificant for four of the six subgroups included in SITC 775 and 881. The opposite is true in the cases of the electric shaver and photographic materials. In turn, trade within SICT 893 is highly concentrated on the subgroup 893.9. The heterogeneous nature of this item suggests that the relatively high intra-industry trade index recorded can be interpreted a result of categorical aggregation.

Table 2.4. Cases of high bilateral intra-industry trade at SITC 3-digit level analyzed by 4-digit groups, 1985. Thousands of current dollars and percentages

SITC	Description and sub-group	Exports[a]	Imports[b]	GL
775	Household type equipment	2295	2528	95.17
	775.2 Refrigerators	0	411	0.00
	775.4 Electric shavers	2295	0	0.00
	775.7 Domestic electrical	0	1354	0.00
	775.8 Electro-thermic	0	763	0.00
881	Photographic apparatus and equipment n.e.s.	187	578	48.89
	881.1 Cameras	14	560	0.05
	881.3 Other photographic equipment	173	18	0.19
892	Printed matter	287	626	62.87
	892.1 Books	257	455	72.19
	892.8 Printed matter n.e.s.	30	136	36.14
893	Articles of plastic n.e.s.	154	585	41.67
	893.9 Miscellaneous plastic articles	154	580	41.96

[a] Argentine exports to Brazil
[b] Argentine imports from Brazil
Source: Own estimations based on COMTRADE data

Thus there is a very great potential for increasing intra-industry trade in consumer goods between Argentina and Brazil. If economic integration is intended to stimulate this kind of trade, policy efforts should be directed to two central aims: reversing the present trend to concentrate bilateral trade flows on a few products, and increasing Argentina's exports to Brazil.

2.3.2.2 Intermediate Goods

Fifty out of the 80 three-digit items which were classified as intermediate goods recorded bilateral trade flows with a total value of more than a $0.5 million (about 0.1 per cent of bilateral trade in intermediate goods). Out of these, 22 observations with low intra-industry indices (less than 40) and trade balances of the same sign in both trade with Brazil and with the world were eliminated. We interpreted this as a signal that bilateral trade flows were governed by the pattern of Argentina's comparative advantages (disadvantages). For the remaining 28 product groups we searched for alternative explanations for intra-industry trade, that is categorical aggregation, vertical specialization, or product differentiation at a more dissaggregative level. This analysis is presented in Table 2.5.

Table 2.5. Argentina-Brazil intra-industry trade indices, 1985. Selected intermediate goods

SITC	Description	Share[a]	GL	H[b]	KR[c]	Dominant
Very High Intra-Industry Trade						
6785	Iron, steel tube fittings	0.15	99.11	H	L	PD
7849	Other motor vehicle parts	15.32	96.59	H	L	PD
8822	Photographic films, plates and paper	3.81	95.33	L	L	I
5239	Inorganic chemical products n.e.s.	0.15	93.04	H	L	PD
5221	Chemical elements	0.41	89.02	H	H	PD/VS
5231	Metal compound of inorganic acids	0.17	88.86	L	H	VS
7492	Cocks, valves etc. n.e.s.	0.38	78.79	H	H	PD/VS
High Intra-Industry Trade						
6251	Tyres, pneumatic, new	0.13	69.71	L	L	I
7491	Ball, roller, etc., bearings	0.24	61.97	L	H	VS
5139	Oxy-function acids and derivatives	0.86	55.01	H	L	PD
7721	Switchgear, etc.	0.67	48.48	H	L	PD
5839	Other polymerization products	1.50	46.81	L	H	VS
5922	Albuminoidal substances; glues	0.16	42.13	H	H	PD/VS
All sampled		23.95				

[a] Percentage of trade in intermediate goods
[b] Hufbauer index
[c] Kol & Rayment index
Source: Own estimations based on COMTRADE data

One observation that can be made from the table is that categorical aggregation associated with statistical aggregation is significant for analysis of intra-industry trade. The sampled three-digit items consisted of a total of 107 four-digit items.

Applying the same criteria as before reduced the number of observations to 39. Of these, a total of 22 yielded an intra-industry trade index with a value of less than 40. As can be observed, the disaggregation of trade data into more narrowly defined categories reduced the number of relevant three-digit items from 28 in the initial sample to 13 in the table.

Drawing on trade data alone, it is a difficult question to determine whether intra-industry trade is a result of product differentiation or vertical specialization. Nevertheless, there are some simple procedures that allow for an indirect approach to the issue. One of these is to proxy product differentiation by the coefficient of variation of export unit values to diverse destinations (Hufbauer index, H in the table). The greater the coefficient, the larger the extent of product differentiation. Another approach, proposed by Kol and Rayment (1989), is to interpret large percentage differences between unit values of imports and exports as an indication of vertical specialization (KR in the table). Both explanations can, of course, be relevant at the same time. However, to the extent that vertical specialization is defined in terms of the fragmentation of a firm's production process on a global basis, it should primarily be seen as a result of the phenomenon of international assembling. Hence, the above stated interpretation of the unit export to import ratio should be considered with some caution when dealing with intermediate goods other than those from the metal-mechanical industry. In the case of chemical products for instance, a significant difference between unit export and import values is more likely to indicate the existence of a technological gap between the two trading economies. This gap would lead firms in the less developed country to specialize in the first processing steps.

Industries in Table 2.5 were ranked according to the GL index and two groups were distinguished, one with high and the other with very high intra-industry trade. In a second step, the ratios described above were computed and then classified into two categories, high and low. The respective means within each group were used as reference values when classifying. Finally we proceeded to identify the dominant source of intra-industry trade, that is product differentiation (PD) or vertical specialization (VS). This is made in the last column of the table. A letter I in that column indicates the indeterminacy which arose when both ratios had low values.

In each of the six cases where vertical specialization constituted an important source of intra-industry trade, either alone or in combination with product differentiation, unit import values were considerably larger than unit export values. Clearly, the sample is too small to draw general conclusions about the nature of the division of labor between the two countries. However, according to the discussion above, one could hypothesize that Argentina tends to produce and export less sophisticated products than Brazil in the case of the four chemical industries. In the case of the two metal-mechanical industries, the hypothesis would be that Argentina is the most favorable location for first processing steps.

2.3.2.3 Capital Goods

As stated earlier, one hypothesis about intra-industry trade in capital goods is that product differentiation increases as a result of technological progress in the sense of further division of labor among firms and larger R & D investments.

Our empirical approach to this issue starts from the assumption that the technological gap between developed and developing economies is larger than that which would result from making comparisons within each group. Accordingly, less developed countries would tend to import the more technologically advanced variety of one product from the more developed countries, while the exchange of the less technologically advanced variety would be mostly confined to trade among developing countries. One should thus expect that intra-industry trade would be more prevalent in Argentina's trade with developing countries than with developed countries. For the latter kind of trade, moreover, we expect that Argentina would be a net importer.

Table 2.6 provides GL indices of intra-industry trade for Argentina's trade in capital goods with Brazil, as well as with the groups of developed (including planned economies) and developing countries (excluding Brazil). As can be observed in the table, the sampled four-digit industries represent more than 39 per cent of total bilateral trade in capital goods.[7]

The classification of industries in the last column is based on the similarities that emerged when comparing the pattern of bilateral trade to the patterns of Argentina's trade with both the group of developed (Dvpd) and developing countries (Dvpg). Criteria for similarity were either a high level of intra-industry trade (above 40 per cent) or a low level of intra-industry trade combined with a trade balance (Argentina's net exports) with the same sign. The words *specific* and *mixed* identify the cases where no correspondence was found or where a double correspondence was found.

A number of observations can be made from the table. First, the average index of intra-industry trade corresponding to Argentina's trade with developing countries is of a relatively higher order of magnitude. Second, in a majority of cases, the pattern of Argentina's trade with Brazil is similar to the pattern it showed with developed countries. As we see in the table, these are all cases of complete or nearly complete specialization, with Argentina as the net importer. For eight of the 10 observations included in this group, discrepancies between the two patterns depend on divergencies in the direction of specialization.

On the basis of the assumptions stated above, one may draw the conclusion that, in these cases, Argentina"s trade with Brazil is dominated by imports of capital goods of a technologically superior quality compared with those produced domestically and exported to other developing countries.

[7] Applying the same selection criteria as in the previous paragraph reduced the number of 3-digit items classified as capital goods from 36 to 13. The latter consisted of 48 four-digit items, of which only 17 exhibited significant (larger than 0.5) percentages of bilateral trade in capital goods.

Table 2.6. Argentina-Brazil intra-industry trade indices, 1985. Selected capital goods

SITC	Description	Share[a]	Brazil		Dvpd		Dvpg		Pattern
			GL	(X-M)	GL	(X-M)	GL	(X-M)	
7223	Track-laying tractors	0.50	0.00	(-)	0.00	(-)	--		DVPD
7423	Rotary pumps nes	2.56	12.18	(-)	0.00	(-)	6.90	(+)	DVPD
7422	Centrifugal pumps nes	1.08	0.00	(-)	0.00	(-)	9.32	(+)	DVPD
7272	Other food-processing machinery	2.07	0.00	(-)	9.38	(-)	13.88	(+)	DVPD
7451	Power tools non-electrical	0.61	0.00	(-)	0.00	(-)	14.41	(+)	DVPD
7421	Reciprocating pumps n.e.s.	0.74	0.00	(-)	0.63	(-)	27.89	(+)	DVPD
7822	Special motor vehicles n.e.s.	0.62	0.00	(-)	0.00	(-)	35.05	(+)	DVPD
6924	Metal transport boxes, etc.	0.61	0.00	(-)	0.00	(-)	35.83	(+)	DVPD
6921	Metal storage tanks, etc.	1.68	0.00	(-)	0.00	(-)	69.90	(-)	DVPD
8748	Electrical measuring equipment n.e.s.	0.50	0.00	(-)	1.04	(-)	79.49	(-)	DVPD
7788	Other electrical machinery n.e.s.	4.49	82.75	(-)	2.16	(-)	44.63	(-)	DVPG
7528	Off-line data processing equipment	13.18	0.00	(-)	0.00	(-)	2.62	(-)	Mixed
6953	Other hand tools	1.29	0.00	(-)	55.19	(-)	38.95	(+)	Specific
7452	Other non-electrical machines n.e.s.	1.69	37.47	(-)	28.98	(+)	2.11	(+)	Specific
8743	Gas, liquid control instruments	1.14	64.34	(-)	3.84	(-)	1.07	(+)	Specific
7525	Adapting peripheral units	1.53	64.49	(-)	37.55	(-)	1.76	(+)	Specific
7431	Pumps for gases, etc.	4.74	93.14	(+)	0.43	(-)	2.07	(+)	Specific
All sampled		39.03	20.84[b]		8.19[b]		24.12[b]		

[a] Percentage of trade in capital goods

[b] Unweighted average

Source: Own estimations based on COMTRADE data

Another large group of industries in the table is composed of industries exhibiting a specific pattern of bilateral trade. In the case of industries numbered 8743 and 7431, both the level of intra-industry trade and the direction of specialization in Argentina's trade with both developed and developing countries suggest the same pattern as before, that is, that Argentina exports the less advanced variety and imports the more advanced variety. In combination with large GL indices for bilateral trade, this indicates a certain degree of complementarity in the exchange of product varieties between the two countries. In the case of the adapting peripheral units industry the GL index for trade with developed countries approaches 40 per cent. This would indicate a greater Argentine contribution to the amount of technical knowledge embodied in the bilateral exchange of product varieties.

One interesting case is the off-line data processing equipment industry, showing the largest share in bilateral trade. As the table demonstrates, this industry is the only one exhibiting a common pattern of intra-industry trade for all the trade flows studied. A closer examination of trade data, however, showed that imports from other developing countries were totally concentrated on Mexico, a country with a level of development comparable to that of Brazil.

2.3.3 Economies of Scale

Among the few empirical studies dealing with the extent of economies of scale in Latin American countries, one of the most valuable is the study by Cline (1982). This author determined the size of the national market relative to the size required for the achievement of efficient production for 18 Latin American countries.

Cline estimated the size of Latin American national markets using 1978 consumption data while he expressed the estimates of the Minimum Optimal Scale (MOS) as percentages of 1967 US consumption. In support of this procedure, he argued that the 1967 US relative factor prices underlying his MOS estimates appropriately reflected the 1978 Latin American relative factor prices. Even so, there is no doubt that this is a very hasty assumption which can only be justified in light of both the shortage of scale-efficiency measures for Latin American countries and his objective of producing estimates for several countries.[8] Here we shall make a tentative analysis for selected consumer and intermediate goods on the basis of the information provided in Table 2.7.[9]

---

[8] Note indeed that MOS estimates are likely to vary among countries. Latin American lower wages for instance can make small old plants operating at scales below the MOS engineering estimates economically efficient. Other factors influencing estimates of the MOS over countries are the size of the country and differences of rules for production (see Pratten, 1988).

[9] Two capital goods industries appearing in the table, however, are ISIC 3831, electric motors, and ISIC 3845, aircraft.

Figures in columns 1 and 2 are percentage shares of MOS in Argentina's and Brazil's 1985 apparent consumption. Apparent consumption has been defined as output plus imports minus exports measured in physical terms.[10]

Table 2.7. MOS as percentage shares of Argentine and Brazilian markets

		1985			1978		
ISIC	Title	Argentina[a]	Brazil[a]	PICEAB[c]	Argentina[b]	Brazil[b]	PICEAB[c]
		1	2	3	4	5	6
3116	Flour mills	n.a	n.a	n.a	11.86	3.15	2.49
3133	Beer brewing	222.85	25.39	22.89	(212.5)82.93	18.89	15.39
3140	Cigarettes	115.94	24.61	20.30	(108.2)89.19	36.67	25.99
3211	Cotton fabrics	n.a	n.a	n.a	3.08	1.12	0.82
3214	Carpets	998.10	1.47	1.47	n.a	n.a	n.a
3240	Footwear	n.a	0.21	n.a	3.64	1.05	0.81
3411	Newsprint	n.a	n.a	n.a	89.80	28.57	21.67
3411	Paper	62.29	13.70	11.23	n.a	n.a	n.a
3511	Sulfuric acid	425.53	27.01	25.40	90.24	31.90	23.57
3512	Fertilizers	202.67	23.18	20.80	n.a	n.a	n.a
3513	Synthetic fibers	48.56	10.60	8.70	n.a	n.a	n.a
3513	Synthetic rubber	191.69	23.69	21.08	(156.7)109.30	32.64	25.13
3513	Cellulose fibers	n.a	n.a	n.a	308.33	92.50	71.15
3521	Paints	45.08	8.99	7.49	n.a	n.a	n.a
3523	Soap	7.97	1.93	1.55	n.a	n.a	n.a
3530	Gasoline	n.a	n.a	n.a	45.24	14.07	10.73
3523	Detergents	311.32	12.55	12.06	(160.0)750.00	17.91	14.46
3551	Tyres	119.55	30.14	24.07	(211.1)108.57	31.15	24.21
3692	Cement	27.60	6.35	5.16	(16.8)200.00	5.48	4.30
3710	Steel	145.56	35.24	28.37	57.78	17.11	13.20
3720	Aluminum	n.a	324.33	n.a	n.a	n.a	n.a
3829	Washing machines	776.70	175.07	142.87	n.a	n.a	n.a
3829	Refrigerators	612.35	51.06	47.13	(576.9)371.05	114.63	87.58
3831	Electric motors	n.a	96.38	n.a	576.92	214.29	156.25
3832	TV sets	183.34	53.16	41.21	n.a	n.a	n.a
3839	Batteries	n.a	34.19	n.a	500.00	15.32	11.73
3843	Automobiles	n.a	n.a	n.a	343.75	103.77	79.71
3845	Aircraft	n.a	n.a	n.a	263.16	80.65	61.73
3844	Bicycles	n.a	n.a	n.a	55.26	11.67	9.64

[a] Own computations based on COMTRADE data and Pratten (1988)

[b] Computed from Cline (1982a) by combining the engineering-based estimates of MOS used by this author with his two different sets of national market size estimates: central estimates for column figures and consumption-based estimates for figures between brackets

[c] Computed as the ratio of the product to the sum of the two countries' percentages

[10] Trade statistics usually report quantity data in tonnes while production statistics often use units and metric measures other than tonnes as area, volume or capacity. Most of the conversion factors were obtained from UN industrial statistics. We also obtained conversion coefficients from Swedish trade statistics (Sweden, 1988) where quantity data in several cases are reported in both tonnes and the other measures.

For a comparison, corresponding percentages based on Cline's central estimates of 1978 domestic consumption are displayed in columns 4 and 5. These are averages of two estimates, one based on production and trade data (apparent consumption) and another derived from a relative (to US) market size function with sectoral income elasticity, relative population and relative *per capita* income as the arguments. Cline used the MOS estimates stated in two studies from the 1970s, Pratten (1975) and Scherer et al. (1975). Estimates used in this paper have been taken from a recent review article (Pratten, 1988). Still most of these are for years before to 1985 and, in some cases they are precisely those used by Cline in his study. This qualifies our (and also Cline's) estimation procedure since, as it is generally acknowledged, the size of the MOS tends to increase over time.[11] Our results reinforce Cline's conclusion that the Brazilian market is large enough to reach MOS for most products. This can easily be verified in the table by comparing 1985 and 1978 percentages in the cases where these two are available. Note in particular the evolution of the refrigerator and electric motor industries with production rising enough during the period to pass the optimal scale level in 1985. With respect to Argentina, the table depicts a number of divergencies between Cline's and our own set of estimates. As the figures between brackets illustrate, most of these divergencies, particularly, the largest ones are probably due to the fact that Cline's income-based and consumption-based estimations gave extremely disparate results. Both sets of estimates lead, however, to the same conclusion, that is, that the Argentine market is too small to achieve MOS for a majority of products.

Columns 3 and 6 show MOS as percentages of the integrated market. These percentages suggest that Argentina would potentially reap large gains from integration in terms of being able to exploit economies of scale. Indeed, according to the table, integration would allow this country to achieve MOS in 14 of the 16 products which, at present, are being produced below optimal scale. For Brazil, on the other hand, the integration of markets would produce this type of scale effects only in the case of the automobile industry.

Notice that the magnitude and distribution of these gains ultimately depend on the effects of both getting access to a broader market and greater competition from the partner country on domestic firms. Some evidence on the issue can be drawn from columns 3 and 6 in Table 2.7. As shown in these columns, the integrated market allows for two or more efficient plants in 24 of the 30 sampled industries. These are the cases for which figures in those columns are equal to or less than 50 per cent. For the remaining six industries, integration of the markets does not preclude the occurrence of inefficiency costs in the form of suboptimal production scale due to either insufficient market size or monopolistic behavior.

---

[11] This can be illustrated by the evolution of plant capacity. In his study of the Latin American fertilizer industry, Patrickson (1990) stated that the smallest designs of new plants available among contractors evolved from 50 to 115,000 tonnes between 1950 and 1990.

In these cases, the most probable outcome of integration would be the exit of firms in Argentina, because it is the country carrying out production at the lowest level below the MOS. Integration would thus reinforce market power for monopolist firms located in Brazil. However, if Argentina has lower costs in one industry, this could induce firms producing for the integrated market to locate there. Moreover, access to the Brazilian market may provide those Argentine firms producing above or close to the MOS incentive to expand in order to reach the MOS or to reap unexploited economies of scale that exist at some range of output above the MOS. Finally, as long as inflation rates and monetary conditions in the two countries continue to diverge significantly, exchange rate pressures can substantially modify the conditions of competition, perpetuating the existence and inefficiency of the marginal firm.

In a long-term scenario of full economic integration with Brazil the real challenge for Argentine industry, however, would be to rationalize structure and modernize production techniques in order to be less vulnerable on the home market to increased competition from Brazilian firms. In addition, such an adjustment would contribute to improving the ability of Argentine firms to meet overseas competition on both the domestic and the world market and thereby to counteract industrialists' pressures for protection.

2.4 Concluding Remarks

This chapter has outlined some of the probable economic effects and problems connected with the implementation of the Trade and Economic Cooperation Program between Argentina and Brazil. Special attention has been paid to three issues: inter-industry adjustments resulting from the liberalization of trade between the two countries, the extent of bilateral intra-industry trade, and economies of scale.

A first and obvious objective of any economic integration agreement would be to immediately eliminate all barriers to trade among participant countries. In the present case, bilateral trade liberalization was to be phased in over several years and priority was given to certain industrial sectors. The objective was to mitigate adjustment costs for domestic firms, in particular those costs resulting from inter-sectoral specialization effects.

In analyzing the direction and intensity of these effects we have focused on sectoral trade data. Two limitations of this analysis are the high level of aggregation used and the exclusion of non-tariff barriers on bilateral trade and tariffs on third parties. The accuracy of our results is also limited by the fact than when relating tariff barriers to a country's comparative advantages, the trade that might have occurred without these barriers has not been taken into account. Hence only tentative conclusions can be stated here. The most important one is that the indiscriminate liberalization of bilateral trade would produce serious adjustment costs for Argentine firms. This supports the view that economic integration between the two countries should proceed gradually and that integration should be aimed at stimulating intra-industry rather than inter-industry trade.

An examination of provisions and instruments of the PICEAB motivated the detailed analysis of bilateral intra-industry trade. Findings from studies dealing with trade liberalization and economic integration under conditions of imperfect competition and product differentiation have provided the theoretical framework for this analysis. Most relevant results relate to trade in differentiated products from the capital goods industries. The pattern of bilateral intra-industry trade found indicates a markedly unequal division of labor between the two countries, with Brazil playing the role of the more technologically advanced country. This raises serious doubts about the adequacy of favoring the capital goods sector in the trade liberalization program as a means of attaining the objective of increased intra-industry specialization.

One of the most powerful arguments for economic integration among developing countries is that very often the size of the country-product market is insufficient to allow MOS plants. The main implication of our analysis of Argentina's and Brazil's market size for consumer and intermediate goods is that under present conditions Argentina would scarcely be able to draw economies-of-scale gains from economic integration with Brazil. Most probably, economic integration would reinforce the position of Brazilian firms on the Argentine market.

3 Patterns of Intra-Industry Trade

From its start, MERCOSUR raised a number of questions about the distribution of the gains and costs of integrating. This was a highly problematic issue on which views diverged considerably. Scholars, for instance, usually approached it in the classic terms of trade creation and trade diversion. Policy-makers and economic actors in turn were rather concerned with the existence of large divergences in economic structure and policy among member countries. In practice, however, the two views pointed to the same issue, namely, the risk of an inefficient reallocation of resources and consumption. This risk was made evident on more than one occasion, when abrupt fluctuations in regional parities, due to divergencies in monetary and exchange policies, caused the trade pattern to deviate from the optimal one associated to tariff elimination. These distortions impacted allocative efficiency negatively by increasing inter-country disparities in firms' competitiveness and unnecessarily amplifying the extent of industrial adjustment.

The integration of national markets, however, can compensate countries for efficiency losses by promoting intra-industry specialization and thereby allowing reductions in average costs and a more efficient allocation of consumption. This is the case, for instance, when market expansion encourages domestic firms to take advantage of unutilized economies of scale and/or scope; or create new opportunities for mergers and joint ventures. International experience in economic integration matters, the European experience in particular, indicates the importance of such effects, which are overlooked in orthodox trade theory, but vital, nonetheless, when evaluating the costs of integration.

Chapter 2 approached the issue by means of an analysis of the benefits of trade in different varieties in the case of Argentina and Brazil. In the present chapter, the analysis is extended to embrace all of MERCOSUR countries. The data used is for the 1975-1990 period and refers, therefore, to the situation prevailing prior to the formation of MERCOSUR. This shortcoming is made up for, in part, in the last section of this chapter, which examines the results of simulating integration-related changes in trade patterns under conditions of imperfect competition and product differentiation. Previously, the more general characteristics of MERCOSUR trade are presented and some methodological issues concerning the measurement of intra-industry trade are discussed. As usual, the analysis of trade flows is confined to the manufactures included in the SITC groups 5 to 8.

3.1 Evolution of Intra-MERCOSUR Trade

During the 1975-1990 period, the average annual growth of intra-MERCOSUR trade in manufactures in current dollars was 8.3 per cent. As evidenced in the last row of Table 3.1, this rate surpassed the corresponding rates for trade between the MERCOSUR countries and other trading partners, namely the member countries of LAIA, EC and the United States.

Table 3.1. MERCOSUR countries. Evolution of total trade, 1975-1990[a]. Rate of growth and percentage distribution by trade partner

	MERCOSUR	LAIA	EC	US	Others	Total
Argentina						
1975-79	14.35	10.26	31.66	19.38	24.36	100.00
1980-84	16.83	6.77	28.43	23.35	24.62	100.00
1985-89	21.02	9.17	25.30	19.37	25.14	100.00
Rate of growth	8.65	3.08	1.32	3.90	3.26	3.48
Brazil						
1975-79	5.51	9.48	30.43	27.82	26.76	100.00
1980-84	7.45	10.74	24.86	27.99	28.96	100.00
1985-89	5.76	8.10	23.71	30.28	32.15	100.00
Rate of growth	7.36	5.04	3.32	6.52	7.97	5.95
Paraguay						
1975-79	82.95	0 .83	6.68	3.91	5.63	100.00
1980-84	85.35	0.48	5.77	3.11	5.28	100.00
1985-89	84.20	0.68	5.07	3.88	6.17	100.00
Rate of growth	7.08	7.73	6.72	9.65	12.76	8.81
Uruguay						
1975-79	60.33	1.90	18.94	10.82	8.01	100.00
1980-84	65.54	1.75	14.42	8.59	9.70	100.00
1985-89	66.72	2.10	13.26	8.89	9.03	100.00
Rate of growth	9.45	8.89	3.90	5.58	7.63	6.94
MERCOSUR						
1975-79	4.00	9.92	32.52	26.52	27.04	100.00
1980-84	5.25	9.84	27.87	27.87	29.17	100.00
1985-89	4.58	8.63	25.58	29.16	32.04	100.00
Rate of growth	8.26	4.57	2.88	5.98	7.01	5.48

[a] Percentages calculated on the basis of total exports and imports accumulated in the periods under review. Rate of growth calculated as indicated in the methodological appendix. For Brazil: 1975-1989

Source: Own estimations based on COMTRADE data

Note, furthermore, that, with the sole exception of Paraguay, this pattern is repeated at the individual country level. The greatest intensification of intra-MERCOSUR trade is recorded in the case of Uruguay, with over 9 per cent, followed by Argentina, Brazil and Paraguay, in that order. Comparison of the rates of growth in the first and last columns of the table provides further information on the issue. Note that the greater the difference between the rate of growth in intra-MERCOSUR trade and the corresponding rate for total trade, the greater the probability of trade deviating toward the region during the period under review. The differences reach a maximum of over 5 percentage points in the case of Argentina, followed by Uruguay with 2.5, Brazil with 1.4 and Paraguay with -1.8, respectively. As a consequence, between 1975 and 1989, the share of intra-MERCOSUR trade in total trade rose by 50 per cent in the case of Argentina and by 10 per cent in the case of Uruguay while it remained almost unchanged in the case of Brazil.

Figure 3.1 illustrates other aspects of intra-regional trade in manufactures, especially the continuous surplus of Brazil in its trade with MERCOSUR partners.

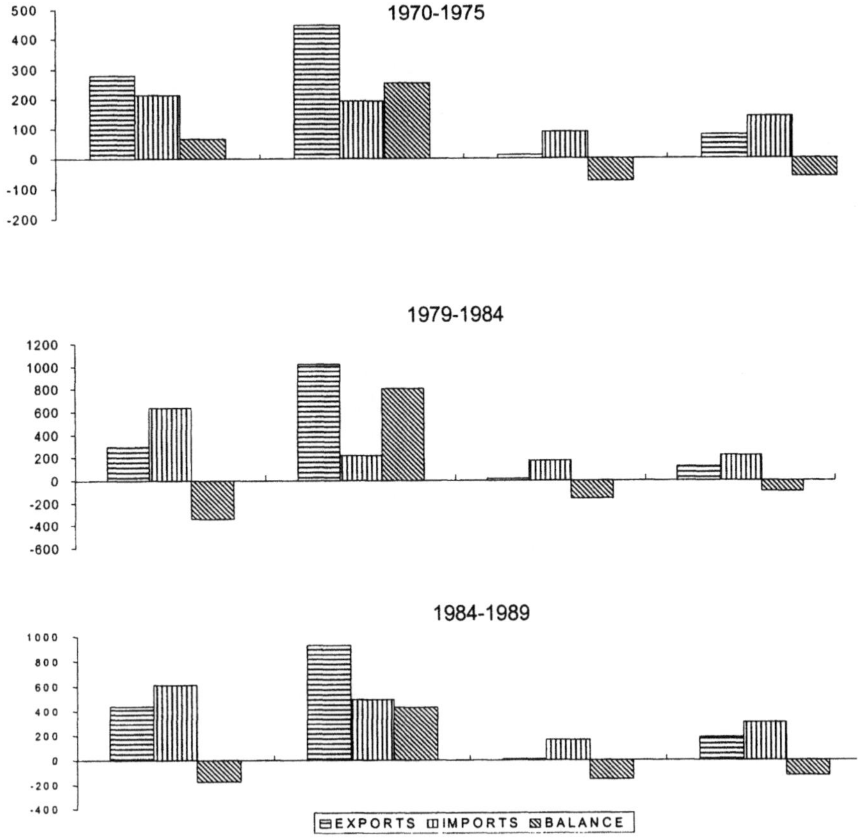

Figure 3.1. Intra-MERCOSUR trade in manufactures. Five-year averages. Millions of current dollars. Own estimations based on COMTRADE data

As reflected in the figure, Brazil showed a trade surplus in the 1975-79 period on the order of $250 million. Most of this surplus was in trade with Paraguay (see Tables A1 and A2 of the Appendix). In the subsequent periods, Brazil's manufactured exports to Argentina increased by more than 300 per cent while imports barely doubled. As a result, Argentina showed an annual deficit in its trade with Brazil on the order of $400 million for the first four years of the 1985-1989 period. This is equivalent to the average Brazilian surplus in intra-MERCOSUR trade during the whole period. This trend was reversed in 1989, basically as a result of the implementation of the PICEAB agreement described in *Chapter 2*, the serious Argentine recession of that year which seriously restricted imports and the reactivation of the Brazilian economy. The fact is, however, that the persistence of that deficit during the relevant period created incertitude about the future of the integration project. Not only because of the cyclical effects on Argentina's balance of payments[1], but more importantly, because of the reaction of the sectors most directly affected.

Table 3.2 below throws more light on the evolution of bilateral flows.

Table 3.2. Percentage shares of bilateral trade flows in total intra-MERCOSUR trade

	Trading partner			
Reporting country	*Argentina*	*Brazil*	*Paraguay*	*MERCOSUR*
Uruguay				
1975-79	**16.22**	**16.12**	**.71**	33.05
1980-84	**12.46**	**14.04**	**.58**	27.08
1985-89	**12.79**	**22.57**	**.32**	35.68
Paraguay				
1975-79	**5.18**	**9.49**	*(.71)*	15.38
1980-84	**3.67**	**10.92**	*(.58)*	15.17
1985-89	**1.80**	**10.58**	*(.32)*	12.70
Brazil				
1975-79	**52.28**	*(25.61)*	.	77.89
1980-84	**58.34**	*(24.96)*	.	83.30
1985-89	**51.95**	*(33.15)*	.	85.10
Argentina				
1975-79	*(73.68)*	.	.	73.68
1980-84	*(74.47)*	.	.	74.47
1985-89	*(66.54)*	.	.	66.54

Source: Own estimations based on COMTRADE data

[1] The Argentine regional trade deficit in manufactures was partially or totally compensated for by the respective trade surplus in primary products.

The figures in bold print indicate the share in percentages of each bilateral flow in total intra-MERCOSUR trade. The sum of these figures together with those between parentheses is, in turn, equal to the participation of each country in the total bilateral flows. These sums figure under the column entitled MERCOSUR. Argentine-Brazilian bilateral trade constitutes the hub of intra-MERCOSUR trade, accounting for 52 per cent of the cumulative total for the 1985-89 period. In order of importance, this figure is followed by Brazil-Uruguay with 23 per cent, Argentina-Uruguay with 13 per cent and Brazil-Paraguay with 11 per cent. The remaining bilateral flows do not reach 5 percent of the total. Note that, with only very minor modifications, this pattern holds for the previous periods as well. The most notable change is visible in bilateral trade between Uruguay and its two largest trading partners. The tendency is one of growing trade between Uruguay and Brazil, at the expense of trade with Argentina.

Table 3.3. Percentage distribution of intra-MERCOSUR exports. According to SITC divisions

Title	1975	1980	1985	1990
Non-electrical machinery	21.90(01)	20.34(01)	15.04(01)	12.94 (01)
Chemical products	4.67(07)	4.97(06)	10.65(03)	12.17 (02)
Transportation equipment	9.63(03)	14.18(02)	10.88(02)	9.06 (03)
Electrical machinery	8.81(04)	9.84(03)	8.74(04)	7.32 (04)
Textiles	6.48(05)	4.17(07)	5.25(08)	6.84 (05)
Basic iron and steel products	11.67(02)	7.48(04)	6.35(06)	6.21 (06)
Plastic materials	1.80(15)	3.13(11)	7.04(05)	5.64 (07)
Other chemicals	2.75(11)	2.37(13)	3.91(09)	4.27 (08)
Leather products	0.75(21)	0.78(21)	5.35(07)	4.17 (09)
Paper	1.97(13)	2.53(12)	2.18(15)	4.09 (10)
Rubber products	2-82(10)	2.15(14)	2.08(16)	3.67 (11)
Metallic mineral products	4.16(09)	4.03(08)	3.29(10)	3.29 (12)
Non-metallic mineral products	6.12(06)	5.31(05)	2.74(12)	3.14 (13)
Paints	0.83(20)	1.08(19)	1.71(17)	2.52 (14)
Miscellaneous products	4.39(08)	3.69(09)	2.50(13)	2.42 (15)
Wearing apparel	2.71(12)	3.47(10)	1.63(18)	2.39 (16)
Basic nonferrous products	1.94(14)	1.21(18)	2.39(14)	2.27 (17)
Instruments, watches, etc.	0.98(18)	1.92(15)	2.80(11)	1.94 (18)
Soaps, detergents, etc.	1.68(16)	1.50(17)	1.54(19)	1.66 (19)
Fertilizers	0.67(22)	0.46(25)	1.06(20)	1.16 (20)
Pharmaceutical products	0.84(19)	0.96(20)	0.96(21)	0.95 (21)
Wood and cork products	1.37(17)	1.68(16)	0.34(24)	0.65 (22)
Footwear	0.15(26)	0.50(24)	0.59(22)	0.48 (23)
Sanitary plumbing, etc.	0.27(24)	0.67(23)	0.25(25)	0.23 (24)
Furniture	0.35(23)	0.76(22)	0.40(23)	0.18 (25)
Travel goods	0.09(27)	0.39(27)	0.04(27)	0.14 (26)
Explosives	0.19(25)	0.41(26)	0.25(26)	0.13 (27)
Petrochemicals	0.00(28)	0.05(28)	0.02(28)	0.07 (28)

Note: The figures in brackets indicate the rank for each year

Source: Own estimations based on COMTRADE data

Table 3.3 provides a complementary picture of the changes that have taken place in the structure of intra-MERCOSUR trade, focusing this time on regional exports. Products have been ranked according to the size of their share in exports for 1990. The figures in brackets indicate the corresponding rank for the product in each year. As can be observed, intermediate and capital goods such as electrical and non-electrical machinery as well as transportation equipment figure among the products that ranked the highest for all years. In turn, the share of chemical exports rose from seventh place in 1975 to second place in 1990. Other export categories that changed place during the period are plastics, which climbed from fifteenth to seventh place and leather products, which climbed from twenty-first to ninth place. The products that showed the greatest decline include metallic and non-metallic minerals. Note, finally, the limited significance of consumer goods such as garments, cosmetics, footwear and furniture in intra-MERCOSUR trade.

3.2 Measurement Problems

The measurement of intra-industry trade has been at the center of an intense debate in the literature on the subject (Greenaway and Milner, 1986). One of the most controversial issues concerns those problems of a statistical nature, which are related to the definition of an industry and referred to as categorical aggregation. Recall from *Chapter 2* that, when measuring the intensity of intra-industry trade in Argentine-Brazilian trade, we first defined "industries" according to the three-digit level of the SITC and found that four such "industries" exhibited high intra-industry trade indices. Analysis at the four-digit level showed just how deceiving these results really were. In effect, at this level, two of the industries – household type equipment and photographic equipment – represented clear cases of next to complete inter-industry specialization. In the plastics industry, on the other hand, there was total concentration of trade in the subgroup denominated "miscellaneous", which includes a wide range of products. It is fitting to point out at this time that none of the available classifications are entirely in keeping with the aims of intra-industry trade analysis (Gray, 1988). Nevertheless, there is a general consensus that, for the purposes of descriptive studies such as the present one, the SITC three- and four-digit classifications allow for a reasonable approximation to the definition of industry (Greenaway and Milner, 1986). The majority of the results presented herein were obtained by applying this criterion, but they will be tested against the results of intra-industry trade measurements based on more rigorous classification criteria.

A second type of problem exists concerning the choice of index. In the majority of the empirical studies on the subject, the index proposed by Grubel and Lloyd (1975) has been employed. This index is arrived at by subtracting from the unit the share of the absolute value of the net trade balance of one industry in the industry's total trade, generally expressed in percentage terms. In accordance with the foregoing, the Grubel and Lloyd (GL) index tends to reach the upper limit of 100 as intra-industry trade increases, nearing zero when the tendency, on the other hand, is toward total inter-industry specialization. In order to avoid the deviation resulting from the presence of trade imbalances, different adjustments to the GL index have been suggested.[2] One such adjustment is the one proposed by Aquino (1978), who assumed that the deviation is distributed proportionately among all the industries.

As concluded by several authors, the type of index selected does not have any major impact on the ranking of the industries according to the magnitude of intra-industry trade (Erzan and Laird, 1984; Tharakan, 1986). In order to test this hypothesis in the case of the MERCOSUR countries, we have calculated the Spearman rank correlation coefficients of the GL and Aquino (Q) indices for three-digit industries, for different years and for different trade flows. The results, which figure in Table A3 of the Appendix, show a high degree of correlation between the ranking of industries according to one index or the other. The value of the coefficients indeed exceeds 0.9 in the majority of the cases of intra-MERCOSUR bilateral trade. Based on the foregoing, we preferred to use the Grubel and Lloyd method to calculate the intra-industry indices at the four-digit level of aggregation, but we will also present the Aquino-adjusted indices as computed at a higher level of aggregation. This will enable us to compare our results with the results of other studies where Aquino-type measurements were employed.

3.3 The Extent of MERCOSUR Intra-Industry Trade

In keeping with that which was set forth in previous sections, the analysis in this section focuses on the intra-industry indices of intra-MERCOSUR bilateral flows. The research is conducted in various stages. First we look at the indices recorded during four selected years and make some comments about the consistency of our results and the hypotheses stated in the literature. Second, we attempt to determine, for each country, the categories of products showing greater intra-industry intensity in the 1975-1990 period. Third, we approach the issue of vertical vs. horizontal product differentiation. As pointed out earlier, Argentine-Brazilian bilateral trade is the hub of integration in MERCOSUR. For that reason we shall explore it in greater detail.

Table 3.4 provides GL indices of intra-industry trade for total manufacture-related transactions within the area for selected years. These indices have been calculated at the four-digit level of aggregation. For the purposes of testing the hypothesis that geographic proximity and/or the presence of trade agreements

---

[2] Greenaway and Milner (1986), however, argue that the direction of adjustment is uncertain and critically dependent on the nature of external equilibrium rather than of imbalance.

Table 3.4. GL Indices of MERCOSUR intra-industry trade by trading partner. SITC 5-8, calculated at the 4-digit level of aggregation.

Trading partner		Reporting country				
		Argentina	Brazil[a]	Paraguay	Uruguay	MERCOSUR[a]
Argentina	1975	.	.	.	.	.
	1980	.	.	.	.	.
	1985	.	.	.	.	.
	1990	.	.	.	.	.
Brazil	1975	24.93	.	.	.	.
	1980	23.83	.	.	.	.
	1985	26.67	.	.	.	.
	1990	53.78	.	.	.	.
Paraguay	1975	0.23	4.03	.	.	.
	1980	3.57	0.11	.	.	.
	1985	2.07	0.06	.	.	.
	1990	1.40	4.84	.	.	.
Uruguay	1975	14.82	3.36	0.00	.	.
	1980	27.18	9.77	0.00	.	.
	1985	24.32	19.06	0.00	.	.
	1990	30.49	21.74	2.42	.	.
MERCOSUR	1975	29.00	27.12	0.25	11.97	.
	1980	40.52	19.72	0.50	27.01	.
	1985	36.20	22.31	0.21	33.80	.
	1990	54.42	41.51	2.57	37.63	.
LAIA	1975	9.77	15.00	0.00	4.03	15.93
	1980	22.65	11.16	0.66	4.89	17.10
	1985	21.97	12.89	0.36	6.14	18.00
	1990	22.98	11.70	3.58	12.28	17.33
EC	1975	8.62	7.89	0.37	0.94	8.77
	1980	8.26	18.78	0.27	3.25	19.56
	1985	11.54	25.45	0.59	4.48	26.46
	1990	26.41	29.69	1.30	5.62	29.97
US	1975	7.83	8.38	0.00	3.03	8.81
	1980	9.90	18.41	0.06	3.53	21.66
	1985	13.91	25.46	0.20	2.63	27.09
	1990	22.30	26.57	2.19	2.76	28.38
Others	1975	8.76	12.57	0.25	1.32	14.58
	1980	8.54	23.17	0.34	4.17	28.79
	1985	16.29	17.69	0.12	5.96	21.13
	1990	19.91	20.61	0.32	9.82	23.01
All	1975	20.80	19.66	1.02	9.59	23.52
	1980	20.95	34.29	0.56	17.49	43.54
	1985	32.29	34.34	0.30	21.82	41.03
	1990	43.19	35.77	2.95	27.55	41.56

[a] The 1990 indices correspond to 1989 data

Source: Own estimations based on COMTRADE data

affect(s) the size of the index, we also look at trade between the MERCOSUR countries and other trading partners.

Note, first, that, for the most part, the intra-industry intensity of Argentine-Brazilian trade is greater than that recorded in other bilateral flows, reaching over 50 per cent in 1990. In that same year, both countries also obtained the highest indices for trade within MERCOSUR, 54 and 42 per cent, respectively, nearing, thereby, the indices recorded for trade among industrialized countries (Greenaway and Milner, 1986; UNIDO, 1993). This is consistent with the hypothesis that the diversification of products and the exchange of product varieties tend to increase the larger the size of the domestic market and the greater the possibility for economies of scale in production. The information provided in the table furthermore confirms the belief that trade liberalization between developing countries intensifies the intra-industry specialization process. Note, in fact, the substantial rise in the indices for 1990, the year in which the integration agreements between Argentina and Brazil, which preceded MERCOSUR by three years, were already in full swing.

Although to a lesser degree than in the previous case, the tendency toward increased intra-industry specialization is repeated in the case of trade between Argentina and Uruguay and in the case of the latter with all of the MERCOSUR members. Note that the Uruguay-MERCOSUR index exceeded 30 per cent in 1985 and, therefore, the average recorded that year for trade between countries with a level of development comparable to that of the MERCOSUR members (UNIDO, 1993). This observation is in keeping with the hypothesis that intra-industry trade is negatively correlated with the distance between trading partners. An additional explanation is the preferential treatment given by Brazil and Argentina to imports from Uruguay since the early 1980s.

Comparison of the intra-MERCOSUR indices with those that figure in the lower panel of the table sheds more light on these aspects. In the cases of Argentina, Brazil and Uruguay, we can see a greater degree of intra-industry specialization in reciprocal trade than in trade with other countries and economic blocs. It is furthermore demonstrated that the indices for Argentina and Uruguay referring to the trade of these two countries with other LAIA members tend to be higher than the indices referring to trade with the EC and the US. The contrary can be observed in the case of Brazil. This is probably due to the greater volume and diversification of extra-regional Brazilian trade as well as to the lesser importance of the LAIA agreements for Brazil as compared to Argentina and Uruguay.

Note, finally, that Paraguayan trade is characterized by a marked tendency toward inter-industry specialization, both in terms of trade with MERCOSUR members and with the remaining trading partners. This observation is in keeping with the hypothesis that intra-industry trade levels are directly related to the concerned countries' degree of development and level of income per capita. The same has been proven empirically on numerous occasions and, more recently, in the case of Latin America (Lord, 1992).

Similar conclusions can be drawn from Appendix Table A5, where the Aquino indices are computed to the three-digit level. These indices are comparable to those calculated by Erzan and Laird (1984) for the 1965-1980 period. Of special interest are the indices obtained by these authors in the case of trade among 10 developing countries, principal exporters of manufactures (PEM), including Argentina, Brazil, Mexico, Yugoslavia and Korea. According to their results, the index in 1980 for that group was 41 per cent, substantially lower than that recorded by Argentina and Brazil in their trade with MERCOSUR members during the same year (56 and 46 per cent respectively) and only marginally higher than that recorded by Uruguay (40 per cent). Moreover, the Aquino index calculated by Erzan and Laird for trade between the PEM group and the group of industrialized countries was 38 per cent – lower, once again, than that of MERCOSUR trade with the United States and equal to MERCOSUR trade with the EC.

Lastly, Figure 3.2 on the next page provides a year-to-year retrospective of the evolution of indices of intra-industry trade for Argentina, Brazil and Uruguay.[3] In the case of Argentina and Uruguay, greater intensity of intra-regional intra-industry trade (MERCOSUR and LAIA) appears to be a constant during the period under review. In the case of Brazil, the evolution of intra-industry trade of the intra-MERCOSUR type tends, on the other hand, to resemble that of trade with the developed countries.

One question that crops up in this context concerns the stability of the specialization pattern when different trade flows are considered. Our computation of Spearman coefficients provided information on the degree of correlation in 1989 between the ranking of the industries according to intra-industry intensity recorded in the exchange among the members of MERCOSUR and that recorded in the exchange with other trading partners. The majority of the coefficients were below 0.5 (see Table A6 of the appendix). Correlation of the 1975 and 1990 rankings of intra-industry trade indices of intra-MERCOSUR trade in turn produced still lower coefficients. These results indicate that there are numerous cases of simultaneous intra- and inter-industry specialization, depending on the direction of the exchange. They further suggest that the dynamism demonstrated by intra-industry trade in the MERCOSUR context does not relate to the increase in product differentiation within a single industry, but to the emergence of specialization processes within new industries.

3.4 Analysis by Product Group

Different hypotheses about intra-industry trade emphasize the technological characteristics of the industries examined. More specifically, it is assumed that intra-industry trade tends to increase in those branches where technological innovation plays a vital role in maintaining competitiveness in the international market. From this perspective, investment in new technologies contributes to

[3] The graph for Paraguay has been omitted since the indices for this country do not exceed 6 per cent in any of the relevant cases.

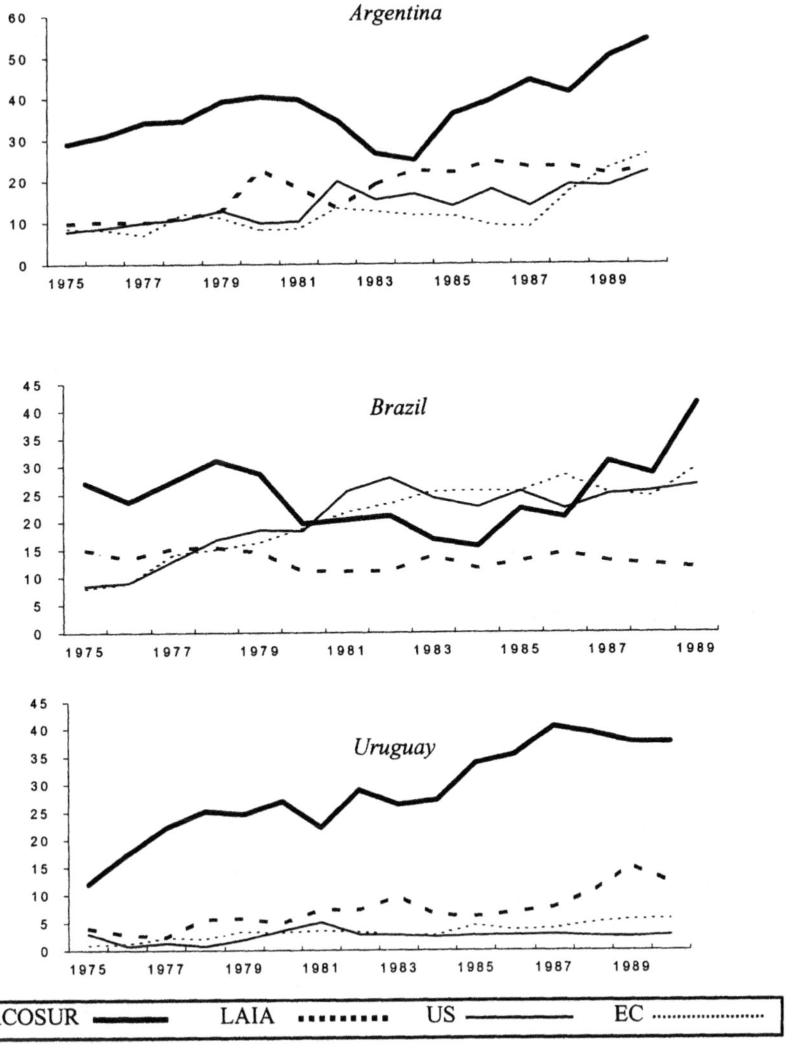

Figure 3.2. Evolution of Intra-Industry Trade Index (GL). 1980-1990. Own estimations based on COMTRADE data

horizontal differentiation of products in the sense that it increases the range of attributes that can be ascribed to a given product, thereby generating new varieties of that product. Likewise, investment in technology intensifies vertical differentiation meaning the development of superior qualities of a given product. Table 3.5 illustrates this aspect in the case of the MERCOSUR countries. The intra-industry trade indices that appear in this table refer to intra-MERCOSUR

Table 3.5. Products with high indices of intra-industry trade in intra-MERCOSUR trade[a]. 1975-1990. Millions of current US dollars

Argentina					Brazil					Uruguay				
SITC	IIT	TT	FI	No	SITC	IIT	TT	FI	No	SITC	IIT	TT	FI	No
8930	89.26	4.5	HC/T	11	8624	82.23	15.3	HC/T	13	7328	87.23	8.7	HC/T	12
7192	83.88	21.1	HC/T	13	7299	81.57	5.6	HC/T	14	5125	83.49	3.4	HC/T	12
6952	81.54	5.5	HC/T	14	7199	81.45	11.6	HC/T	12	7199	79.86	2.6	HC/T	11
7199	80.74	13.1	HC/T	14	5995	81.34	3.0	HC/T	8	5142	79.38	2.4	HC/T	12
7115	79.95	21.6	HC/T	9	5333	80.85	6.9	HC/T	9	5811	77.99	8.3	HC/T	12
7143	79.06	9.9	HC/T	12	5142	80.73	3.1	HC/T	9	6535	77.63	3.1	UL	10
8624	77.71	15.2	HC/T	14	7231	77.85	3.3	HC/T	13	5121	76.50	4.4	HC/T	9
7221	77.23	4.9	HC/T	10	7143	77.24	11.3	HC/T	11	6114	75.19	5.8	NR	11
5995	76.91	3.5	HC/T	9	5310	76.53	2.1	HC/T	9	5813	74.08	2.3	HC/T	12
7328	76.09	66.7	HC/T	15	7328	76.53	50.3	HC/T	12	7231	72.75	4.0	HC/T	12
7299	75.09	6.1	HC/T	15	6554	75.46	3.3	UL	9	5812	69.11	1.7	HC/T	11
7196	73.75	6.3	HC/T	9	7192	74.66	21.7	HC/T	13	8930	68.98	3.2	HC/T	12
8619	69.94	3.1	HC/T	11	7250	74.54	12.4	HC/T	12	6770	66.95	1.9	HC/T	9
7193	69.53	3.8	HC/T	10	7196	73.65	7.6	HC/T	9					
5999	69.41	8.9	HC/T	11	8921	73.37	2.8	HC/T	10					
7222	68.57	6.6	HC/T	14	8619	73.08	2.9	HC/T	11					
8921	65.69	5.8	HC/T	9	6952	72.92	5.4	HC/T	12					
					5125	72.49	12.1	HC/T	12					
					5999	70.74	9.9	HC/T	10					
					6291	68.86	28.7	HC/T	9					
					5542	65.96	6.2	HC/T	9					

IIT, intra-industry trade index; TT, total trade; FI, factor intensity; HC/T, human capital and technology; UL, unskilled labor; NR, natural resources

[a] Averages calculated on product groups with more than one million traded dollars and indices over 50% for 9 or more years

Source: Own estimations based on COMTRADE data

trade flows. They have been calculated at the four-digit product group level and are based on data for the 1975-1990 period. Only those recording more than one million traded dollars and indices over 50 per cent for nine or more years during said period were considered. Each one of the groups thus selected has been classified in the columns entitled FI according to factor intensity. Three categories of products have been considered: human capital- and technology-intensive (HC/T), intensive in unskilled labor (UL) and natural resource-intensive (NR).[4]

All of the 17 products selected in the case of Argentina were classified as intensive in human capital and technology. The proportions were 20 out of 21 for Brazil and 11 out of 13 for Uruguay. Paraguay did not record any group of products that met the criteria established above. Note that in the three countries the products with the highest amount of intra-industry trade (over 80 per cent) belong to the HC/T category. In the case of Argentina, these groups of products are the following: plastics (8930), pumps and centrifuges (7192), tools (6952) and machinery parts and accessories (7199). In the case of Brazil, photographic equipment (8624), diverse electrical appliances (7299), once again machinery parts and accessories, gluten and other products (5995), paints (5333) and inorganic acid compounds (5142). Lastly, in the case of Uruguay, automobile parts (7328) and organic acids (5125).

Generally speaking, the predominance of products classified as intensive in human capital and technology confirms the hypotheses that stress the importance of economies of scale and differentiation processes induced by technological change for intra-industry trade. The status of intermediate and capital goods of said products however calls for a more cautious analysis. Recall from *Chapter 2* that the sources of intra-industry trade in intermediate products and capital goods differ in general from those of consumer goods. According to the data furnished in that chapter, the 14 intermediate goods industries which in 1985 recorded intra-industry indices over 50 per cent for Argentine-Brazil trade falls under the HC/T category. Of these, six represent potential cases of product differentiation (vertical or horizontal). In another six cases, however, vertical specialization, in the form of international fragmentation of the production process, appears as a relevant explanatory factor. It was also demonstrated that Argentine-Brazilian trade in capital goods was dominated by Brazilian exports of the most advanced varieties.

In certain industries producing finished goods such as paints (5333), detergents (5542), and electrical appliances (7250), there is a greater likelihood of the high indices of intra-industry trade reflecting "true" cases of horizontal differentiation, in the sense of consumers' preference and differences in product attributes. Note, however, that the indices in the table refer to multilateral flows. As mentioned before, these indices may be illusory when it comes to bilateral flows.

---

[4] The relationships between this classification and the SITC may be consulted in Appendix Table A7.

3.5 Vertical Differentiation *versus* Horizontal Differentiation

As pointed out earlier, the problems of categorical aggregation in the measurement of intra-industry trade do not disappear simply because the measurement has been carried out at the four-digit product group level, as is the case in the present study. Obviously, one way of overcoming this limitation is to resort to less aggregate data. This would furthermore allow for greater accuracy in the measurement of trade in horizontally differentiated products. The availability of data, however, sets precise limits on this type of empirical exercise. In the present case, the limit is the five-digit groups established by the SITC. At this level of aggregation the analysis can differentiate between similar products such as tools for processing nonmetallic products and those used in the lumber industry. Even so, the differences in export and import values, due either to differences in transportation costs or in the quality of the marketed products, could introduce a deviation in the measurement of intra-industry trade, and confuse the cases of horizontal differentiation (HD) with those of vertical differentiation (VD). To avoid problems of this nature, we have used the criteria established in a recent study (Abd-el Rahman 1991). When applied to the groups of five-digit products, these criteria lead to the classification of trade according to the categories specified in Table 3.6, enabling us to obtain a more exact approximation of the different forms of trade in the MERCOSUR countries.

Table 3.6. Definition of categories employed in the classification of trade flows

1 -way, inter-industry	digit groups where the value of exports (imports) is less than 10 per cent of the value of imports (exports).
2-way, intra-industry vertical differentiation	5-digit groups in which significant export and import flows are recorded but in which the difference between the unit values of exports and imports is over 15 per cent
2- way, intra-industry horizontal differentiation	5-digit groups in which significant export and import flows of products of equal quality (namely unit differences of less than 15 percent) are recorded.

Table 3.7 details the results from classifying the total and intra-regional trade of the MERCOSUR countries according to the categories enumerated above. These results can be compared with the GL indices that figure in Table 3.4. Both in the case of total and intra- regional trade, the percentages for two-way trade (HD + VD) tend to be higher than the GL indices. Note, however, that according to the table a good part of this two-way trade originates in the exchange of products differing in quality (VD). With the exception of the percentages for Uruguay at the beginning of the period, the share of this type of exchange in total

Table 3.7. Percentage distribution of total trade in manufactures by type of trade. SITC 5-8, calculated at the 5-digit level of aggregation

	Total trade					Intra-MERCOSUR trade				
	One way	Two-way vertical	Total	Two-way horizontal Bilateral	Two-way horizontal Multilateral	One way	Two-way vertical	Total	Two-way horizontal Bilateral	Two-way horizontal Multilateral
1975										
Argentina	72.88	21.75	5.36	3.68	1.68	52.58	40.23	7.19	3.12	4.07
Brazil	74.90	23.50	1.61	0..91	0.70	65.25	27.29	7.45	6.03	1.42
Paraguay	98.21	1.67	0.12	0.07	0.06	99.63	0.37	0.00	0.00	0.00
Uruguay	85.57	4.63	9.80	7.95	1.85	80.45	6.34	13.21	8.46	4.75
1980										
Argentina	67.96	25.86	6.19	3.51	2.67	48.08	43.50	8.42	1.52	6.89
Brazil	51.74	44.75	3.51	1.48	2.03	74.53	20.04	5.43	3.03	2.41
Paraguay	99.00	0.97	0.03	0.00	0.03	99.02	0.92	0.06	0.04	0.02
Uruguay[a]	77.06	n.a	n.a	n.a	n.a	69.48	n.a	n.a	n.a	n.a
1985										
Argentina	56.22	35.31	8.47	3.71	4.76	44.88	45.24	9.87	1.57	8.31
Brazil	50.40	45.13	4.46	2.99	1.47	68.02	26.78	5.20	1.11	4.10
Paraguay	99.87	0.07	0.06	0.06	-0.00	99.99	0.01	0.00	0.00	0.00
Uruguay	71.37	13.72	14.92	7.77	7.15	65.10	18.01	16.90	4.98	11.92
1990										
Argentina	37.12	54.54	8.34	6.49	1.85	36.79	37.49	25.72	19.27	6.45
Brazil[b]	43.70	55.19	1.11	1.03	0.09	35.67	55.01	9.32	4.32	5.00
Paraguay	95.47	4.52	0.01	0.00	0.01	95.41	4.04	0.55	0.00	0.55
Uruguay	66.41	26.01	7.58	5.77	1.81	59.21	34.76	6.03	1.80	4.22

[a] Data concerning import quantities were not available for this year [b] 1989
Source: Own estimations based on COMTRADE data

trade tends to substantially exceed the trade in HD products. The share of the latter in intra-MERCOSUR trade fluctuates between 7 and 26 per cent for Argentina, 5 and 9 per cent for Brazil, and 6 and 17 per cent for Uruguay.

These low percentages of trade in HD products, together with the predominance of capital and intermediate goods, suggest that consumers' preferences have played only a limited role in the generation of MERCOSUR intra-industry trade. This is confirmed by comparing said percentages with those obtained for countries such as France, where it is assumed that demand characteristics play an important role in the generation of intra-industry trade. In this case, in effect, it has been demonstrated that the share of trade in HD products in total trade with other EC members totals 46 per cent, exceeding the share of trade in VD products by more than 10 percentage points (Abd-el Rahman, 1991).The growth in trade in VD products is very pronounced in the case of Uruguay. Between 1975 and 1989, this participation rose from 5 to 26 per cent of total trade and from 6 to 35 per cent of intra-MERCOSUR trade. With some fluctuations, this tendency is repeated in the case of Brazil, where the respective increases are on the order of 32 and 28 percentage points. The distribution by trading partner of bilateral intra-MERCOSUR trade in HD products which figures in Table 3.8 complements the information provided in Table 3.7. The growing importance of Brazil for Uruguayan trade in such products is evident in the table. In 1975, trade with Brazil accounted for a meager 10 per cent of Uruguayan trade in HD products with the region.

Table 3.8. Percentage distribution of bilateral intra-MERCOSUR trade in HD products by trading partner. SITC 5-8, calculated at the 5-digit level of aggregation

		Argentina	Brazil	Paraguay	Uruguay
1975	Argentina	0.00	99.45	0.00	0.55
	Brazil	99.54	0.00	0.17	0.28
	Paraguay	0.00	0.00	0.00	0.00
	Uruguay	90.34	9.66	0.00	0.00
1980	Argentina	0.00	83.15	0.00	16.85
	Brazil	95.20	0.00	0.00	4.80
	Paraguay	100.00	0.00	0.00	0.00
	Uruguay[a]	n.a	n.a	n.a	n.a
1985	Argentina	0.00	63.23	0.00	36.77
	Brazil	95.53	0.00	0.00	4.47
	Paraguay	0.00	0.00	0.00	
	Uruguay	58.46	41.54	0.00	0.00
1990	Argentina	0.00	98.60	0.05	1.35
	Brazil[b]	60.57	0.00	2.19	37.24
	Paraguay	0.00	0.00	0.00	
	Uruguay	4.59	95.30	0.10	0.00

[a] Data concerning import quantities were not available for this year

[b] 1989

Source: Own estimations based on COMTRADE data

Since 1975, Brazilian participation has been doubling every five years, reaching 95 per cent in 1990. Note that the role of Argentina as an Uruguayan trading partner in this type of trade tends to diminish symmetrically.

3.6 The Impact of Regional Integration

The reciprocal tariff-reduction schedule established by the Treaty of Asuncion provides for the dismantling of intra-MERCOSUR trade barriers in 1996. The agreement furthermore provides for the derogation of multiple administrative norms and state regulations impeding the free flow of goods between the member countries. This package of liberalizing measures should stimulate intra-regional trade and the search for economic efficiency, which would obviously mean greater gains for both consumers and firms. The final distribution of these gains will depend, however, on the inevitable industrial adjustment that will result from the formation of the common market. As pointed out in *Chapter 2*, the costs of this adjustment could be mitigated if it takes place in the context of growing specialization and intra-industry trade. This depends, among other things, on prior industrial protection levels, the extent of economies of scale and demand characteristics. In this section we take a look at these aspects based on the results of the partial equilibrium model which is presented in *Chapter 5*. For the purposes of calibration five trading partners were considered: Argentina, Brazil, Uruguay, the rest of LAIA and the rest of world. Paraguay was included in the rest of LAIA because of the lack of sufficiently disaggregate production data.

Table 3.9 provides some of the characteristics of the industries selected for the base year used in the calibration of the model.

The Herfindal index in the fourth column of the table indicates the (pre-integration) degree of market concentration when the sales of foreign firms are considered in addition to those of local firms. The higher the index, the higher the degree of concentration and therefore the lower the level of competition. The last three columns provide the structure of total trade in each industry by destination. As can be observed, these structures differ dramatically from one another. In the electrical household appliances industry (3833), for example, the average share of intra-MERCOSUR trade in the total trade of the three countries is over 40 per cent. In the pharmaceutical industry (3522), this share does not reach 9 per cent.

Table 3.10 compares the intra-industry trade indices resulting from the simulations with the pre-integration indices resulting from the calibration of the model. Observed intra-industry indices at the base year are displayed in Table A8 (Appendix). For the purpose of analyzing the table, we define the type of specialization in an industry as predominantly inter-industry or intra-industry based on whether the respective GL index is under or over 50 per cent. The following conclusions can be drawn directly from the table:

In the group of industries composed of synthetic fibers, pharmaceutical products, clay products and office machinery, the 50-per cent reduction in

Table 3.9. Some characteristics of selected industries, 1985. Millions of current dollars and percentages

Country ISIC	Production	No of Firms	Herfindal index	Total trade	Percentage of total trade MERCOSUR	LAIA	Others
Argentina							
3513	280.00	11.00	.07	68.77	16.89	30.76	52.35
3522	1253.93	48.00	.09	113.42	6.24	7.06	86.69
3691	178.65	48.00	.02	18.91	11.28	1.21	87.51
3825	164.43	5.00	.03	265.69	6.46	7.59	85.95
3831	200.00	35.00	.03	84.79	8.51	4.04	87.45
3833	358.00	12.00	.24	11.21	52.28	8.51	39.21
3843	3155.00	5.00	.18	292.69	25.40	13.12	61.48
Brazil							
3513	1884.00	17.00	.05	202.51	5.28	10.16	84.56
3522	3072.37	68.00	.07	170.11	3.66	8.76	87.58
3691	1557.88	28.00	.04	53.43	4.80	20.11	75.09
3825	2481.97	43.00	.04	431.96	4.10	7.00	88.90
3831	3151.83	73.00	.02	380.93	3.31	6.74	89.94
3833	1871.40	18.00	.17	41.76	10.63	16.25	73.12
3843	16300.00	7.00	.14	1477.44	5.77	15.46	78.77
Uruguay							
3513	32.00	4.00	.13	17.37	66.01	2.29	31.70
3522	116.59	25.00	.15	20.77	14.44	5.09	80.48
3691	5.38	10.00	.06	3.92	39.13	3.42	57.45
3825	2.58	11.00	.01	8.36	16.67	4.00	79.33
3831	8.91	24.00	.01	13.09	74.42	0.87	24.70
3833	30.00	6.00	.39	5.80	58.48	0.72	40.80
3843	71.31	4.00	.13	30.18	77.98	0.16	21.86

Source: Chapter 5.

reciprocal tariffs tends to increase Argentine-Brazilian intra-industry trade. In the other three industries, that is, electrical machinery, electrical household appliances and motor vehicles, on the other hand, the indices fall dramatically. Note that, in the case of synthetic fibers, the index rises from 32 to 59 per cent, thereby reverting the type of specialization in the inter-intra direction. In the case of electrical household appliances, however, the type of specialization moves in the opposite direction, intra-inter, with the index falling from 58 to 26 per cent.

The total elimination of tariff barriers in the second panel of the table accentuates the foregoing tendencies. This is particularly the case in the motor vehicle industry where the index falls to less than 33 per cent, reflecting a lower level of intra-industry specialization when trade between both countries is liberalized. It should be pointed out, however, that the foregoing observation is based on the assumption that trade flows are entirely governed by market forces – a notion which is rather questionable in the present case given the importance of sectoral and intra-firm trade agreements in the MERCOSUR automobile industry. Note, furthermore, the sizeable increase in the GL index in the office machinery industry associated with the establishment of a free trade zone. In keeping with the

Table 3.10. Impact of regional integration on intensity of intra-industry trade

Bilateral trade	Synthetic fibers 3513		Pharmaceutical products 3522		Bricks & clay products 3691		Office machinery 3825		Electrical machinery 3831		Electrical household appl. 3833		Motor vehicles 3843	
	Pre	Post	Pre	Post	Pre	Post	Pre	Post	Pre	Post	Pre	Post	Pre	Post
Experiment 1: 50% reduction in intra-MERCOSUR tariffs and 50% increase in LAIA preferences														
A-B	32.05	58.69	3.94	5.39	3.31	6.08	7.04	18.67	95.21	71.48	58.19	25.52	88.88	53.95
A-U	48.14	51.80	6.90	6.45	44.51	68.51	10.71	9.59	21.88	15.72	16.35	44.02	64.60	37.48
B-U	97.10	82.14	14.02	17.32	76.38	90.15	1.93	11.03	65.48	57.49	4.13	5.16	0.24	0.29
A-MS	39.64	57.08	57.09	61.41	13.05	16.90	11.87	23.83	73.87	59.87	96.21	47.23	87.02	53.25
B-MS	63.70	74.21	5.76	7.73	35.12	45.92	6.75	18.15	82.29	98.23	89.88	61.81	89.08	73.24
U-MS	71.38	68.09	9.46	10.41	99.05	97.95	4.66	10.60	55.24	46.58	78.04	68.89	16.36	8.64
Experiment 2: 100% reduction in intra-MERCOSUR tariffs and 100% increase in LAIA preferences														
A-B	32.05	89.25	3.94	7.05	3.31	9.34	7.04	39.79	95.21	54.35	58.19	10.71	88.88	32.87
A-U	48.14	57.81	6.90	6.07	44.51	61.77	10.71	9.59	21.88	12.42	16.35	88.98	64.60	20.65
B-U	97.10	67.05	14.02	20.67	76.38	66.99	1.93	32.76	65.48	54.14	4.13	6.50	0.24	0.33
A-MS	39.64	85.93	57.09	65.46	13.05	16.57	11.87	44.35	73.87	48.47	96.21	17.48	87.02	32.59
B-MS	63.70	96.00	5.76	9.91	35.12	71.80	6.75	39.26	82.29	81.09	89.88	38.02	89.08	45.18
U-MS	71.38	63.42	9.46	11.47	99.05	66.28	4.66	26.40	55.24	42.33	78.04	37.00	16.36	4.88

A, Argentina; B, Brazil; U, Uruguay; MS, MERCOSUR

PRE, results from calibrating the model, assuming conditions of imperfect competition in prices (Bertrand)

POST, results of simulations assuming a constant number of firms

Source: Chapter 5

results of the simulations, growing intra-industry trade in this case is associated with greater penetration of Argentine firms into the Brazilian market. The synthetic fibers industry provides a symmetrical example of the above. In this case, the pre-integration tariff differences are small, whereas the average size of the Brazilian firm considerably exceeds that of its Argentine equivalent. As a result, the share of Brazilian firms in the Argentine and Uruguayan import markets increases, without these firms suffering any major losses in their own market (see *Chapter 5* for more details). The indices of bilateral flows between Uruguay and its two trading partners figure under the heading U-MS. As can be observed, the 50-per cent tariff reduction affects the GL indices to a lesser degree than in the case of Argentine- Brazilian trade.

The type of specialization only changes direction in the case of the electrical machinery industry, where the tendency is toward inter-industry specialization, but this tendency is marginal since the index hovers around the 50-per cent mark. Generally speaking, total tariff elimination does not change the foregoing industrial specialization model to any great extent. The exception is the electrical household appliance industry, whose index falls from 59 to 33 per cent. The breakdown of this index by bilateral flows suggests, however, marked intensification of intra-industry trade with Argentina.

The case of Uruguay is particularly interesting given the small size of its domestic market and the consequent smaller average size of its firms. Because of these factors, a greater impact on production and more extensive industrial adjustment can be expected. This is particularly true for the four electro-mechanical branches: office machinery, electrical machinery, electrical household appliances and motor vehicles. In these industries, and particularly in the last two, the integration process tends to reduce the participation of Uruguayan firms in the local market without the increase in its exports compensating totally for these losses. Consequently, production levels drop dramatically and average costs increase.[5]

The electrical household appliances industry provides a good illustration of the changes in industrial specialization, which may be induced by the integration process. As highlighted earlier, integration produces a strong increase in the intensity of Uruguayan intra-industry trade with Argentina in that industry. The presence of this phenomenon, alongside the fall in the level of production in Uruguay, is related, on the one hand, to the increased inter-penetration of both markets. On the other, it relates to the fact that Uruguayan firms lose a vast proportion of their own market as a result of a sizeable increase in imports from Brazil. In the context of the model, this is interpreted as a process in which Uruguayan firms tend to specialize in some competitive variety in the Argentine market while the varieties sold locally are displaced by Brazilian equivalents and, to a lesser degree, by Argentine varieties.

---

[5] The latter due to the hypothesis of economies of scale.

3.7 Conclusions

The conclusions of this study can be summarized as follows:

Over the course of the last fifteen years, intra-regional trade in manufactures between the MERCOSUR member countries has increased considerably. Generally speaking, this increase has exceeded that of all other trade flows, which suggests that greater inter-penetration of local markets has actually taken place. This trend predates the entering into effect of the Treaty of Asuncion and is clearly favorable for the integration process that is currently under way. The persistence of serious imbalances in the trade of manufactures between Argentina and Brazil, which constitutes the hub of MERCOSUR integration, may however have serious implications for the future of the integration project. Accordingly, there is a pressing need for greater coordination in matters of monetary as well as exchange rate policies, in addition to policies concerning the dismantling of non-tariff barriers and the move towards a common tariff. All of the above would provide a more adequate framework for the trade liberalization process, reducing distortions in relative prices and thereby facilitating increased competitiveness and intra-industry specialization.

The present study has analyzed the prospects for such specialization based on retrospective analysis of intra-industry trade. At the most general level of the analysis, it was first confirmed that the better part of intra-regional trade was concentrated on intermediate products and capital goods. Second, it was demonstrated that the ranking of the different industries, according to the intensity of intra-industry trade, was not overly affected by variations in measurement procedures.

Comparison of intra-industry trade indices, according to country type and trading partner, allowed us to test our findings against a series of hypotheses as stated in the literature. First, it was shown that, in keeping with the theory maintained by different authors, the two larger economies showed the highest indices of intra-industry trade both in the case of intra- and extra-MERCOSUR trade flows. Second, it was shown that in the case of Argentine-Brazilian bilateral trade, the index rose rapidly in 1990, nearing the levels observed in trade between developed countries. The fact that the process of reciprocal tariff reduction launched between Argentina and Brazil preceded that of MERCOSUR by several years is consistent with the hypothesis that integration agreements encourage intra-industry trade. The hypothesis tends to be corroborated as well in the case of trade between Argentina and LAIA countries. Data for Uruguay further confirm the notion that intra-industry trade is negatively correlated with distance and enhanced by lower trade barriers. Indeed, the intra-industry indices for this country in its trade with MERCOSUR partners were higher than indices corresponding to its trade with other countries and to trade between developing countries with a similar degree of industrialization as Uruguay. The clearly inter-industry nature of Paraguayan trade, for its part, corroborated the hypothesis that this type of trade is associated with lower levels of income and economic development.

The analysis further revealed that in the case of Argentina and Uruguay the greater intensity of intra-industry trade in trade with MERCOSUR partners was a constant during the period under review. It was also confirmed that the direction of trade modified the trade pattern, with numerous cases of simultaneous intra- and inter-industry specialization appearing according to the type of flow examined. Finally, it was confirmed that the increase in intra-industry trade within the MERCOSUR context was associated with the emergence of new specialization processes.

The disaggregate analysis demonstrated that, in intra-MERCOSUR intra-industry trade, the groups of products which predominated were those which were highly human capital and technology-intensive. This corresponds with hypotheses linking intra-industry trade to product differentiation resulting from technological innovation and economies of scale. Analysis at the most disaggregate level possible confirmed the importance of intra-industry trade for MERCOSUR countries but indicated that a good part of that trade was due to the exchange of vertically differentiated products, that is, products differentiated by quality. The low levels in percentage terms of trade in horizontally differentiated products and the small share of consumer goods in intra-MERCOSUR trade suggest that, contrary to the industrialized countries, factors on the demand side play a minor role in the process of intra-industry specialization among MERCOSUR countries.

Results from a simulation model in which economies of scale and product differentiation were taken into account, indicated that the impact of integration on the intensity of intra-industry trade differed from one industry to another. The magnitude and the direction of these effects depended on pre-existing levels of economies of scale in production, the degree of tariff protection and relative plant size. Taking the MERCOSUR as a whole, integration raised the level of intra-industry specialization in four of the industries considered and lowered it in the other three. At the bilateral level, however, it was demonstrated that while integration led to losses in domestic market shares, it also offered new opportunities for specialization through penetration of associated markets.

4 Plant-Size Effects of Trade

Previous chapters focussed on MERCOSUR countries' trade pattern and explained it in the light of theoretical approaches that emphasize the role of economies of scale and product differentiation. In the present chapter, the focus is on the opposite question, namely how trade can promote the fuller exploitation of economies of scale.

It is expected that trade liberalization and the integration of national markets into a regional one will facilitate the attainment of minimum efficient plant size (MES) for local firms. It is also expected that the establishment of a common (and lower) external tariff will provide a more competitive framework for domestic producers and stimulate their search for cost efficiency. Even if these expectations are well grounded in economic theory and experience, the recognized multiplicity of factors behind observed plant-size differentials among industries and across countries gives us sufficient reason to test the underlying hypothesis; that is, that trade flows influence firm's choice of plant size to some extent and in a specific direction. The aim of this chapter is to provide empirical evidence on this issue for three of the MERCOSUR countries, namely, Argentina, Brazil, and Uruguay.[1]

4.1 Differences in Plant Size

Table 4.1 shows the distribution of manufacturing plants and employment by size of plant, which prevailed in the three countries in different years.[2] In order to make these industrial structures comparable, the data refer to plants with twenty or more employees. As it emerges from the table, Brazil displays the largest deviation from an equal distribution of manufacturing employment, followed by Argentina and Uruguay, in that order. Brazil is also the country with the largest concentration of both employees and firms in the two middle-size groups when these groups are considered together (100 to 499 employees).

[1] Data on Paraguay, the fourth country, were not reliable or not available.
[2] The selection of the years of reference was determined by the availability of census data.

Table 4.1. Comparison of industrial structures by employment-size class. Selected MERCOSUR countries, percentages

	Uruguay - 1978		Argentina - 1984		Brazil - 1985	
Size class	Employees	Plants	Employees	Plants	Employees	Plants
20-49	17.6	53.1	16.1[a]	49.8[a]	14.8	52.1
50-99	18.8	25.1	16.6	25.8	14.3	22.2
100-199	18.9	12.5	16.9	13.2	24.9[b]	16.8[b]
200-499	20.9	6.6	23.3	8.4	20.0[c]	6.1[c]
500 and over	23.8	2.7	27.1	2.8	26.0	2.8

[a] Size class 25-49

[b] Size class 100-249

[c] Size class 250-499

Source: Own computations based on census data

Table 4.2 provides a more meaningful picture of inter-country differences in plant size. Diverse measures of national representative plant size are given and compared in the table. Note first that the larger the country is, the larger the overall manufacturing ratio, defined as the ratio of total manufacturing employment to the number of manufacturing plants. According to the table, the Brazilian ratio is double the Argentine and more than triples the Uruguayan ratio. Two other ratios, which summarize the structure of size-differentials by industry in some way, are shown in the table. They are the average plant size and the Top 50 index, the latter being defined as "the average size of plants comprising the upper half of an industry's sales or employment size distribution" (Scherer and Ross, 1990). As can be seen in the table, the means of both the average plant size

Table 4.2. Comparison of plant employment sizes. Computed at the 4-digit level of the ISIC. Selected MERCOSUR countries

	Uruguay - 1987		Argentina - 1984		Brazil - 1985	
	Mean	Median	Mean	Median	Mean	Median
Normal plant sizes						
OR	9.0	---	13.0	---	27.0	---
AV	23.4	11.5	46.3	18.8	51.0	42.7
TOP50	189.1	78.9	354.1	149.7	367.0	366.0
RPS	20.6	18.5	22.3	14.9	14.2	12.8
Size comparison of						
OR	69.2	---	100.0	---	207.7	---
AV[a]	71.3	59.0	100.0	100.0	224.4	179.4
Top 50[a]	91.3	56.5	100.0	100.0	538.1	181.8

OR, the ratio of total manufacturing employment to the number of manufacturing plants; AV, the ratio of an industry's employment to the industry's number of plants; TOP50, computed as explained in the text; RPS, the percentage share of average plant in TOP50

[a] Comparison performed at the industry level

Source: Own computations based on census data

and the Top 50 index are considerably smaller for Uruguay than for Argentina and Brazil. Note further that, when the comparison is performed at the industry level, the Brazilian average Top 50 index becomes more than five times larger than the Argentine and Uruguayan ones. Finally, note that, when the comparison is related to the median which is not influenced by extremely large values of the ratios, the magnitude of the divergence between Argentina and Uruguay grows to more than 40 per cent for both the Top 50 index and the average plant. Relative plant size figures in the table are percentage shares of average plant in Top 50. The corresponding mean ranges from a magnitude of 14.2 in the case of Brazil to 22.3 for Argentina. When the comparison is related to the median, Uruguay moves to the first position in the ranking.

4.2 Factors Determining Production Scale

As stated before, the main hypothesis to be tested in this chapter is that trade influences plant scales. The test will be performed within the framework of an econometric model, but prior to specifying its functional form and examining the empirical results, it seems appropriate to begin with a short discussion of both the variables included and the economic rationale of underlying assumptions.

The most complete study of the determinants of plant size is perhaps the one performed by Scherer et al. (1975). The study classifies the factors influencing decisions into two main groups of variables designated location and market variables and forwards a number of hypotheses about their relationship with the deviations of representative plant size from minimum efficient scale plant size. Applying a multiple regression model to a pooling sample of twelve industries and six countries then tests the theoretical assumptions. Representative plant size is measured by Top 50, all the variables being computed in physical terms.

Most of current studies in the field, including the present one, derive their approaches from the work referred to above. Because of limitations either in data availability, research time or both, only a subset of the independent variables mentioned above are included in the empirical analysis. By the same reason, the multi-country approach is usually avoided, and shortcut methods are often adopted when computing a proxy for the dependent variable. Table 4.3 summarizes some of the features of the basic model in the form originally specified by Scherer *et al.* (1975) and compares it with later versions of the same model as formulated by Müller and Owen (1985), Schwalbach (1988), Helg and Ranci (1988), and the author himself.

As shown in the table, the main differences among the models refer to the approach to the dependent variable and the selection of independent variables. Both issues are related to the way of measuring the variables, either in physical or in value terms, and to the ensuing data problems.

Table 4.3. Models of plant size determinants. Some characteristics of the studies quoted

Study	Scherer et.al	Müller & Owen	Schwalbach 1	Schwalbach 2	Helg & Ranci	Behar 1	Behar 2	
Dependent variable	TOP50/MES	TOP50/MES	AV/MES	AV/TOP50	AV/MES	AV/MES	AV/TOP50	
Measurement	Physical	Physical	Physical	Values	Physical	Physical	Values	
Cross-sectional	Multi-country							
model	Multi-sector	Multi-sector	Multi-sector	Multi-sector	Multi-sector	Multi-sector	Multi-sector	
No. of countries	6	1	2	2	1	2	2	
No. of sectors	12	20	22,19	103,105	14	15,22	66,79	
Location variables								
	Production costs	X	X	X	---	X	X	---
	Transport costs	X	---	---	---	---	--	---
	Demand density	X	---	---	---	---	---	---
Market variables								
	Size	X	X	X	X	X	X	X
	Concentration	X	---	---	X	---	---	X
	Trade	X	X	X	X	X	X	X
	Other	X	---	---	---	---	---	---
Other variables								
	Output growth	---	---	---	X	---	---	---
	Labor productivity	---	---	---	X	---	---	X
	Multiplant operation		---	---	---	X	---	------

X, variable included; ---, variable excluded

The measurement of variables in physical terms affects the analysis in two ways. On the one hand, it improves the reliability of the results as the MES estimates used in the computation of the dependent variable can be made available from engineering studies. On the other hand, the representativeness of the results is limited by the fact that MES estimates are available only for a small number of product lines. Besides, there is the difficulty of obtaining size-distribution data at the product-line level in order to compute variables such as industrial concentration and even the Top 50 index. Note that in three of the studies where the analysis is performed in physical terms (Schwalbach 1, Helg & Ranci, and Behar 1), the latter index has been substituted with the average plant when computing the dependent variable, while four of the models omit the concentration variable.

Measuring variables in value terms from census information considerably alleviates data problems and improves the representativeness of the results, but it sacrifices the reliability of the MES estimates and precludes the use of the associated cost gradient variable. The approach in this case consists of approximating the MES using the Top 50 index. The latter has been proposed in the literature as a good substitute to the former (Scherer and Ross, 1990) and can be derived from census data either in employment or in output terms. The dependent variable is then computed as the ratio of the average plant to the Top 50 index. This is the procedure followed in Schwalbach 2, and Behar 2. Finally, the decision to incorporate other variables into the model is greatly dependent on balancing research time and data availability with the objectives of the study. In this chapter, the emphasis has been put on the role of market variables, that is trade and domestic consumption variables. Hence, we shall concentrate in the following on the hypotheses related to these variables and make short comments on the remaining selected variables.

4.3 The Rationale of the Variables Included in the Model

4.3.1 Trade Variables

The direction of causality is a central problem that requires a closer examination in any empirical exercise. As regards the export variable, all the above mentioned authors assume in principle that the expansion of exports stimulates the building of larger plant in the same way that growing domestic demand does. The issue is of great interest to developing countries where capacity subutilization and suboptimal capacity is a widespread phenomenon due to the limited dimensions of domestic demand. It would apply in particular to small open economies or to large countries, which are attempting to implement trade liberalization policies as a way of overcoming internal constraints and improving economic efficiency. In these cases, export expansion is more likely to raise the actual level of capacity-utilization at the plant level and to enhance the firms' perceived market, stimulating investment decisions directed to increase capacity. According to this, lower levels of suboptimal capacity could be expected in those industries showing larger export to output ratios.

Yet, most of the authors remark the importance of feedback effects. Scherer and others (1975), for instance, recall that since export markets are highly competitive, export performance and size-related cost efficiency are likely to interact as constitutive elements of a "whole process (which) is surely a gradual, cumulative one". Helg and Ranci (1988) go further in their critical appraisal of the issue. They point out that conclusive theoretical evidence in the field of industrial organization is not to be found about the causal link between the two variables, export intensity and plant size, and that the same applies to other variables such as industrial concentration.

While it seems that the role of exports can clearly be stated on a priori grounds, the role of imports becomes uncertain in the present framework. In fact, the hypotheses stated in the literature suggest an ambivalent role for imports as regards their impact on the building of larger plants. On the one hand, there is the hypothesis that increased imports would have a negative impact on relative plant size. Adapted to the conditions prevailing in Latin American countries, the central argument here would be that a highly protected home market leads domestic firms to perceive the market as a captive one. In periods of rapid domestic demand growth, this not only provides opportunities of higher profits but also encourages large-scale investments since local firms are not afraid of losing market shares to foreign competitors. This assumption seems to apply well to the pattern of industrial development as followed by Argentina, Brazil, Uruguay, and other Latin American countries during the earlier phases of the import-substitution period.

There is reason, however, to question the above stated market contraction hypothesis. It should be doubly qualified in the present case. First, the lack of import competition should be recognized as having played a completely different role during the earlier phases of the import substitution period. Indeed, when some degree of market control arises and firms adopt some form of oligopolist strategy, they may become unwilling to search for cost efficiency. Second, economies of scale have a dynamic, which requires an aggressive investment policy. This policy may be disregarded when competition is lacking. Plants which at the earlier phases of import substitution might be close to the MES become clearly suboptimal at latter stages. Higher import exposure may counter this trend by forcing domestic firms to improve efficiency.

In summary, two hypothesis are stated concerning the import variable: the market contraction hypothesis, which states that increased import penetration in one industry would reduce the likelihood for the industry's representative plant to reach the efficient scale; and the import competition hypothesis, which postulates the converse effect.

4.3.2 Cost and Market Size

Two additional variables in our regression models are the cost gradient and the market size variable.[3] For both variables, the hypothesis is that the larger they are, the greater the incentive to build larger plants and thus, the larger the ratio of representative plant size to the MES. Certainly, the increase of average costs due to sub-optimal plant size would indeed be amplified in those industries showing steeper unit cost curves, and the risk of sub-optimal production scale would be augmented when the domestic market is not large enough to support a single MES plant (see *Chapter 2*).

4.3.3 Market Concentration and Labor Productivity

Market concentration and labor productivity may also influence relative plant size. As regards market concentration, one hypothesis is that firms operating in a highly concentrated market are more likely to believe that their market shares will be maintained when demand shifts than firms operating in a more competitive market would. As a consequence, the former would be more willing to expand capacity in existing plants in order to meet a presumptive demand increment. Multiplant operation is a widespread phenomenon, however, and the risk of variable misspecification does exist if market concentration is measured on a plant basis as we do in this paper due to data constraints. Finally, a positive relationship between labor productivity and relative plant size is expected, but the direction of causality again is not clear. Low labor productivity may indeed accentuate propensities toward investment in small plants, particularly in the case of labor-intensive industries located in countries that face a low wage/rent ratio. At the same time, however, it seems reasonable to expect larger output per worker ratio for those industries where cost efficient plants prevail.

4.4 Data Sources and Model Specification

As stated above, the availability of data governed our choices concerning the method of computing the variables and the set of variables included in the estimations. Data problems also explain the selection of the base years.

In the cases of Argentina and Brazil, we first proceeded at the product-line level with the variables being measured in physical terms and, then, at the industry level with the variables being measured in value terms. Base years for the former analysis were 1983 and 1980, respectively. The magnitude of MES and cost gradient variables was derived from engineering studies published in diverse

[3] Recall that these two variables can simultaneously be included in the estimations in a consistent way only when they are measured in physical terms and the analysis is performed at the product-line level (model 1 in Table 4.3).

studies,[4] while production and trade data came from miscellaneous sources.[5] Since no data of physical output were available for Uruguay, the analysis for this country had to be performed solely at the industry level.[6]

The literature offers no clear guidance as to the appropriate functional form of the plant size determinants model. Accordingly, our selection was rather guided by the statistical properties of the samples.[7] Both a multiplicative and an additive model were specified and estimated. Examination of the distribution of regression residuals provided the primary criteria for selecting one or the other specification. The testing showed that the additive model was the most appropriate one when the variables were to be measured in physical terms, whereas the multiplicative model was the most appropriate one when variables were to be measured in value terms. The full specifications were formulated as follows:

$$PSD_i = a_0 + a_1MS_i + a_2CU_i + a_3EI_i + a_4II_i + u_i, \tag{4.1}$$

for variables measured in physical terms and

$$PSD_i = a_0\, a_1\, MS_i\, a_2\, CU_i\, a_3\, EI_i\, a_4\, II_i\, u_I, \tag{4.2}$$

for variables measured in value terms. In this case, the model was estimated linearly in the logarithms.

The dependent variable was defined as shown in Table 4.3 while the independent variables were as follows:

- *MS*;. market size, measured by the ratio of domestic consumption to the MES alternatively the Top 50 index. Domestic consumption was computed as output+import-export.
- *CU*; the cost gradient, defined as the increase in unit costs at 1/3 of MES.
- *PROD*; labor productivity, measured by the ratio of output to the number of employees.
- EI; the export intensity measured by 1+exports/output
- *II*;. the import intensity measured by 1-imports/domestic consumption.
- *CONC*;. market concentration, measured by the Herfindahl index on an employment basis[8].

---

[4] The increase in costs at lower than MES are for 1/3 MES. Both MES estimates and the estimates of the increase in costs were obtained from Pratten (1987), Pratten (1991), and Schwalbach (1988).

[5] Mainly publications by national and international statistical offices and diverse reports published by local corporations and Chambers of Commerce.

[6] We used published census data for the years 1978 and 1988 in the case of Uruguay, and unpublished census data for the years 1984 and 1985 in the cases of Argentina and Brazil, respectively.

[7] This is also the approach adopted by authors like Scherer et al. (1975) and Schwalbach (1988).

[8] The 1978 Herfindahl indices for Uruguay were taken from Buxedas and Roca (1984) while the 1988 index for Uruguay and indices for Argentina and Brazil were computed on census data.

In order to estimate the impact of intra-MERCOSUR trade on plant size deviations from the MES, two additional variables in value terms were defined;

- *EIR*;. the intra-MERCOSUR export intensity measured by 1+intra-MERCOSUR exports/total exports.
- *IIR*.; The intra-MERCOSUR import intensity measured by 1-intra-MERCOSUR imports/total imports.

A positive sign was expected for the coefficients of all the dependent variables, excluding import variables. For the latter variables, the coefficient was expected to be positive if the market contraction hypothesis was true and negative if the competition hypothesis was true.

4.5 Empirical Issues and Regression Results

4.5.1 Product Lines

4.5.1.1 Argentina

The correlation matrix (see Table A12) reveals the existence of a strong correlation between the two dependent variables *MS* and *CU*. This may imply multicolinearity problems in the estimation of model specification (regression (1)). As can be observed in Table 4.4, the adjusted regression coefficient for the complete version of the model (regression (2)) amounts to 0.7.

Omitting *CU* from the estimation as in regression (1) increases the regression coefficient by 0.017 and does not affect the values and the signs of the other individual coefficients to any considerable extent. Apparently, *CU* is a superfluous variable without any independent influence on *PSD*. Among the other variables, market size is by far the most important one. As shown by regression (3), this variable provides more than 90% of the explanatory power of the regression.

Table 4.4. Results for the regression additive model Argentina 1983

Equation	(1)	(2)	(3)
Constant	-0.248	-0.252	0.019
MS	0.039[c]	0.046[c]	0.039[c]
CU		-0.158	
EI	0.142	0.141	
II	0.131[a]	0.149[a]	
Adj. R^2	0.721	0.704	0.693
No of observations	15	15	15

[a] Significant at 10% level

[b] Significant at 5% level

[c] Significant at 1% level

Finally, note that while there is some evidence that trade variables influence plant size decisions this influence is relatively weak

4.5.1.2 Brazil

No correlation among the dependent variables was detected in this case. With the exception of *CU*, all the coefficients were statistically significant at the levels equal or lower than 10 per cent. Again, the importance of market size is verified. This variable captures more than 70 per cent of the explanatory power of the regression. Of the two trade variables, the one showing the strongest explanatory power is import intensity with its coefficient being statistically significant at the 5 percent level.

Table 4.5. Results for the regression additive model. Brazil 1980

Equation	(1)	(2)
Constant	0.118	0.120
MS	0.060[c]	0.040[c]
CU	-1.688	
EI	2.581[a]	
II	-2.727[b]	
Adj. R^2	0.442	0.314
No of observations	22	22

[a] Significant at the 10% level
[b] Significant at the 5% level
[c] Significant at the 1% level

4.5.2 Industry Level

As shown in the appendix Tables A13 to A16, multicolinearity may be a problem in our samples. We proceed by steps, beginning with the uncorrelated variables and taking into account both the stability of the estimated coefficients and the increment in R^2 when deciding to incorporate remaining variables into the equation.

4.5.2.1 Argentina

Table 4.6 reports the estimated parameters for three specifications of the multiplicative model. The effect of multicolinearity is made visible when comparing regression (2) with (3). Note the instability of the coefficients of trade variables when the two strongly correlated variables *MS* and *CONC* (cf. Table A13) are simultaneously taken into account. Multicolinearity may be causing the recorded notable increase in the values of the coefficients.

Table 4.6. Results for the regression multiplicative model Argentina 1984

Equation	(1)	(2)	(3)	(1A)
Constant	-2.015[c]	-2.992[c]	-2.088[c]	-2.141[c]
MS		0.204[b]	1.170[c]	
CONC			1.114[c]	
PRODUCT	0.068	0.064	0.112	0.045
MS.CONC	1.143[c]			0.985[c]
EI	2.328[b]	0.643	2.421[c]	
II	1.077[c]	0.075	1.016[c]	
EIR				0.291
IIR				0.094
Adj. R^2	0.455	0.018	0.453	0.372
No of observations	79	79	79	78

[a] Significant at the 10% level
[b] Significant at the 5% level
c Significant at the 1% level.

In (1), the two correlated variables have been replaced by their product.[9] Comparing (1) and (3) throws light on the role of the interactive variable leading to a higher R^2 and to a non-adjusted R^2 (not reported) only 0.004 less than in (3). Besides, the signs of the coefficients of the trade variables are not affected.

Table 4.7. Results for the regression multiplicative model Argentina 1984

	Consumer goods		Capital goods	
	(1.1)	(1.1A)	(1.2)	(1.2A)
Constant	-3.080[c]	-2.835[c]	-1.472[c]	-1.726[c]
PRODUCT	-0.200	-0.214	0.206	.0.242
MS.CONC	1.029[c]	0.898[c]	0.161[c]	0.907[c]
EI	3.945[b]		1.553	
II	0.438		1.191[b]	
EIR		0.230		0.092
IIR		0.340[b]		-0.380[a]
Adj. R^2	0.442	0.398	0.458	0.415
No of observations	43	43	36	36

[a] Significant at the 10% level
[b] Significant at the 5% level
[c] Significant at the 1% level

[9] Examination of the correlation matrix (not reported) showed that the new interactive variable was not correlated with any other of the remaining independent variables.

Regression 1 was therefore used as the basic model when regressing the regional specification of the trade variables (1A) or when partitioning the sample into two groups of goods, that is, consumer and capital goods. The latter estimations are displayed in Table 4.7.

Note, finally, that the signs of the coefficients of market size and trade variables remain stable when moving from the product-line level (Table 4.4) to the industry level (Table 4.6).

4.5.2.2 Brazil

As shown in appendix Table A14, two pairs of variables were correlated in this case; namely, *MS* and *CONC* and the latter and *PROD*. Compare now the results of regressing uncorrelated variables exclusively (regression 2 in Table 4.8) with the ones corresponding to regression (3) where all variables are taken into account. Multicolinearity may be the main factor behind the considerable reduction in the absolute value of the coefficient of the import variable. It may also be the cause for this coefficient to lose statistical significance in regression (3). Finally, note the changes in the coefficients of the size and export variables, particularly the change in the sign of the latter.

Substituting *MS* and *CONC* for their product notably attenuates multicolinearity effects. The coefficient of the import variable indeed remains statistically significant and the sign of the one of the export variable unchanged. Note further that the latter coefficient becomes statistically significant at the 10 per cent level. This suggests that, as in the case of Argentina, equation 1 provides the most adequate model for the analysis of the impact of trade variables on plant

Table 4.8. Results for the regression multiplicative model. Brazil 1985

Equation	(1)	(2)	(3)	(1A)
Constant	-1.302[a]	-1.234[a]	-1.682[c]	-1.143[c]
MS		0.045	0.911[c]	
CONC			0.896[c]	
PRODUCT	0.330[c]	0.517[c]	0.274[c]	0.399[c]
MS.CONC	0.839[c]			0.399[c]
EI	-0.711[a]	-0.144	0.331	
II	-1.302[a]	-2.338[b]	-0.904	
EIR				-0.164
IIR				-0.089
Adj. R^2	0.675	0.183	0.689	0.491
No of observations	70	76	69	73

[a] Significant at the 10% level
[b] Significant at the 5% level
[c] Significant at the 1% level

size. The results of applying this model to regional variables and specific groups of goods are found in Table 4.8 (regression 1A) and Table 4.9, respectively.

Table 4.9. Results for the regression multiplicative model. Brazil 1985

	Consumer goods		Capital goods	
	(1.1)	(1.1A)	(1.2)	(1.2A)
Constant	-2.005[a]	-1.920[a]	-1.146[b]	-0.872[b]
PRODUCT	0.153	0.197	0.385[c]	0.491[c]
MS.CONC	0.802[c]	0.555[c]	1.018[c]	0.800[c]
EI	-0.888[a]		-0.033	
II	-2.054[a]		0.267	
EIR		0.152		-0.047
IIR		-0.202		-0.177
Adj. R^2	0.623	0.330	0.747	0.655
No of observations	38	39	32	34

[a] Significant at the 10% level
[b] Significant at the 5% level
[c] Significant at the 1% level

4.5.2.3 Uruguay

Appendix Tables A15 and A16 report a strong inter-correlation among *PROD*, *MS*, and, *CONC* for the 1988 sample and between pairs of variables such as *MS* and *CONC*, *MS* and *EI*, and *PROD* and *CONC* for the 1978 sample.

Table 4.10. Results for the regression multiplicative model. Uruguay 1988

Equation	(1)	(2)	(3)	(4)	(5)	(1A)	(2A)
Constant	-1.625[c]	-3.143[c]	-1.553[b]	-1.936[c]	-1.217[b]	-1.019	-1.186
MS	0.345[c]	0.161	0.348[c]	1.331[c]	1.331[c]	0.520[c]	0.534[c]
CONC				1.268[c]	1.164[c]		
PROD	0.494[c]		0.507[c]		0.260[a]	0.749[c]	0.761[c]
EI		0.176	-0.262	1.767[b]	1.412[c]		
II	-0.437[b]	-0.440[b]	-0.446[b]	0.689[c]	0.594[b]		
EIR							0.397
IIR						-0.080	-0.106
Adj. R^2	0.212	0.107	0.200	0.451	0.468	0.253	0.248
No of obs.	63	63	63	63	63	54	54

[a] Significant at the 10% level
[b] Significant at the 5% level
[c] Significant at the 1% level

Variables in regression (2) are *MS*, which showed the highest correlation coefficient with the dependent variable, and two other uncorrelated variables, namely, *EI* and *II*. Incorporating *PROD* into the regression as in (3) does not affect the sign of the coefficient of *II*. Moreover, both the magnitude and the significance level of the coefficient remain almost unchanged. The sign of *EI* does change in the wrong direction but the coefficient is not statistically significant in either (2) or (3). Note, finally, that the coefficients of *MS* and *PROD* get the expected sign and are statistically significant at the 1 per cent level. Compare now these results with those emerging from regression (5) where all the relevant variables are taken into account. The value of R^2 increases by more than 100 per cent in relation to (3) and all the coefficients become significant; but now the detrimental effect of multicolinearity is becoming apparent. Note in particular the strong increase in the coefficients of *MS* and *EI* and the reversal in the sign of *II*. These effects are preserved when *PROD* is dropped as in (4) indicating that, as could be expected, the main source of multicolinearity problems is the interaction of *CONC* and *MS*.[10] Comparison of (1) and (3) finally suggests that variable *EI* has no independent influence on *PSD*. Dropping EI indeed increases R^2 slightly from 0.210 to 0.212.

The pattern described above applies to a great extent to the 1978 regressions (Table 4.11) and to a specification of the 1988 equation based upon intra-MERCOSUR trade variables instead of total trade variables (regressions (1A) and (2A) in Table 4.10). In the latter case, however, neither of the coefficients of the two trade variables is statistically significant.

Table 4.11. Results for the regression multiplicative model . Uruguay 1978

Equation	(1)	(2)
Constant	-5.961[c]	-3.830[c]
MS	0.237[b]	1.265[c]
CONC		1.243[c]
PROD	0.656[c]	0.422[b]
EI	1.819[a]	3.064[c]
II	-0.120	0.940[b]
Adj. R^2	0.151	0.340
No of observations	49	49

[a] Significant at the 10% level
[b] Significant at the 5% level
[c] Significant at the 1% level

[10] In an attempt to avoid these problems, we used the CONC.MS interactive variable instead of its two components. The results (not reported here) were unsatisfactory. The new variable was highly correlated with the import variable and the reversal in the sign of the latter sustained.

The correlation matrix again indicates a risk for unreliable coefficients due to multicolinearity problems. The stepwise procedure, however, shows that the repercussions of the statistical interdependence of variables are not as serious a problem as in the previous case. Further emphasis is on the role played by the interaction between *MS* and *CONC*.

4.6 Analysis of Results

In the following, the analysis will mainly be related to the regressions labeled (1) and (1.) in Tables 4.4 through 4.11. The results of the estimations confirm the hypothesis that variations in relative plant size across industries or lines of products are strongly associated to differences in market size. The regression coefficients for this variable either when acting in isolation or in combination with the concentration variable are of the expected positive sign and significantly different from zero at the 1 or 5 per cent level.

The coefficient of the cost gradient variable does not show the expected sign in either the Brazilian or the Argentine regression. The coefficients lack statistical significance, but the occurrence of the negative sign in both regressions is still disturbing. The evidence provided by other studies does not help further in understanding such a crucial issue. Müller and Owen (1985), for instance, get a positive scale coefficient from their 1965 Germany regression but a negative one from the 1980 regression. Schwalbach (1988) in turn reports a negative parameter for the United Kingdom in 1982 and a positive parameter for Germany in 1965 and 1982. Finally, Helg and Ranci (1988) produce a positive coefficient when working with Italian data but it is not statistically significant.

The coefficient of the export variable appears with the expected positive sign in all the Uruguayan and Argentine regressions. It becomes statistically significant at the industry level in both the 1978 Uruguayan regression and the 1984 Argentine regression. These results suggest that growing exports are efficient in stimulating the building of large plants in both countries. However, note that for Uruguay the importance of exports decreased between 1978 and 1988. On the whole, the results for Brazil indicate a complex relationship between plant size and export orientation. The coefficient of the export variable appears with the expected sign and is statistically significant at the 10 per cent level in the product-line level regression but it gets the wrong sign in nearly all the industry-level regressions. It is negative and statistically significant at the 10 per cent level in the regressions corresponding to the application of the basic model to both the whole sample and the sample of consumer good industries. This suggests the existence of diseconomies of scale in export activities, especially in the export of consumer goods.

With respect to the import variable, we note first that the results from the Argentine estimations are consistent with the market reduction hypothesis. The coefficient appears with a positive sign and is statistically significant in both the industry and the product-line estimations. The import competition hypothesis is instead true in the cases of Uruguay and Brazil. The coefficient of the import variable receives a negative sign and is statistically significant at the 5 per cent level in both the 1980 (product line level) and 1985 (industry level) Brazilian regressions and in the 1988 Uruguayan regression. The comparison of the latter with the 1978 regression further suggests that the influence of Uruguay's imports on plant size increases over time. In contrast to their Argentine colleagues, industrialists in Uruguay and Brazil seem to have a competitive perception of their domestic market and tend to build larger plants as import exposure increases.

Focusing on the intensity of intra-MERCOSUR trade was not particularly enlightening for the total sample of industries. The coefficients of regional trade variables got the same signs as the ones for total trade variables but they were not statistically significant. More interesting information could be obtained when the Argentine sample was partitioned into two sub-samples according to the type of good produced, capital or consumer goods. In the case of capital goods, the coefficient of the intra-MERCOSUR import variable got the negative sign and was statistically significant at the 10 per cent level. The conclusion here is that the Argentine firms, which operate in the capital goods sector, react competitively to imports from partners, mainly Brazil, by seeking for size-related cost efficiency. Note that this is not the case for the sector's total imports. Exports to partners in turn do not seem to have any measurable effect on the behavior of firms in either the capital goods or the consumer goods sector. The lack of statistical significance of regional trade variables in the Brazilian regressions does not allow for drawing any conclusion on the impact of these variables on plant size, neither at the level of the whole sample or at the level of the two subsamples.

The independent explanatory power of the productivity variable is evident in the Uruguayan and Brazilian regressions. In both cases, the relevant coefficient is positive and statistically significant. The partitioning of the Brazilian sample into two sub-samples throws more light on the issue. The relevant coefficient becomes statistically significant only in the case of the capital goods sample. Less clear is the role of this variable in the Argentine regressions. The coefficients do get the expected positive sign for the entire sample of industries but are not statistically significant. Moreover the sign of the coefficient is negative in the case of the consumer goods regression.

Finally, the coefficient of the market concentration variable is highly significant in the 1978 Uruguayan regression but, as already mentioned, multicolinearity problems led to the rejection of a specification including this variable in both the 1978 and the 1988 regression. Its effects could not be disentangled from those of the market size variable in the Argentine and Brazilian regressions by the same reason.

4.7 Concluding Remarks

This chapter has focused on one of the dimensions of economies of scale, namely, plant size and its relationship with trade. Our analysis tends to give a positive answer to the main question stated in the introduction: Do trade flows influence relative plant size in MERCOSUR countries?

The analysis shows that higher export intensity lead to the construction of larger plants in Argentina and Uruguay, thus contributing to the achievement of scale economies in these countries. In the case of Brazil, the analysis revealed a complex relation between plant size and export intensity with the results pointing to the existence of both a positive and a negative relation between these two.

The analysis also indicates that inter-industry differences in import exposure have sizeable effects on plant scales but that the nature of these effects varies from one country to another and from one sector to another. Furthermore, our results provide some insight into the question posed in this chapter about the ability of Argentine firms to retain market shares in the context of an integrated market. The question has particular connotations for Argentine firms operating in the capital goods sector for two reasons: Brazil's recognized comparative advantages in capital goods and the fact that this sector was the first industrial sector to be selected for integration when trade negotiations between the two countries began in 1986 (Cf. *Chapter 2*). The results suggest that when the level of import exposure increases, Brazilian and Uruguayan firms react by building large plants while Argentine firms in general adopt a defensive policy by reducing scale. Evidence on the capital good sector, however, indicates that increased import competition from Brazilian firms operating in that sector may stimulate scale investment by Argentine firms.

Table 4.12. Percentage changes in relative plant size produced by a ten-percent increase in trade. Selected countries

Country	Exports	Imports	Total trade
Germany[a]	8.5	16.5	25.0
United Kingdom[a]	19.4	4.1	23.5
Italy[b]	21.2	-5.8	15.4
Argentina[c]	0.9	-2.1	-1.2
Brazil[d]	4.3	2.7	7.0

[a] 1982

[b] 1982-83

[c] 1983

[d] 1980

Source: Schwalbach (1988), Helg and Ranci (1988) and own computations

As a last illustration of the effects of trade flows on plant size, Table 4.12 provides estimates of percentage changes of the dependent variable when import and export intensity increases by a 10 per cent at the average level and all the other independent variables remain unchanged. Figures in the table were computed by using the Brazilian and Argentine regression estimates related to model specification (1) with variables measured in physical terms. For a comparison, percentage changes corresponding to three European countries are also shown in the table.

According to the table, a ten-percent increase in trade intensity reduces the relative plant size by 1.2 per cent in the case of Argentina and increases it by 7 per cent in the case of Brazil. These are very marginal effects as compared with those computed for the EC-countries displayed in the table.

5 Cooperation and Competition
Industry Simulations of Trade Liberalization

The main purpose of this chapter is to investigate the effects of reciprocal tariff reductions for three of the four Latin American countries which form the MERCOSUR, namely Argentina, Brazil, and Uruguay. The study is conducted within the framework of the partial equilibrium model developed by Smith and Venables (1988). The model, which allows for economies of scale and trade in differentiated products, has previously been used to analyze the effects of the completion of the EC (Smith and Venables, 1988), the resource and welfare implications of Spain's access to the EC (Gual, Martinez Giral and Vives, 1989), and the likely effects of EFTA (European Free Trade Association) countries' joining the Community (Norman, 1989). It has also been applied to the study of optimal tariffs and subsidies for industrialized countries (Gasiorek, Smith, and Venables, 1989). As far as we know, the present study is the first attempt to apply the Smith-Venables model to data on developing countries. Next sections describe the model and the calibration procedure, makes some short comments on data-related problems and examine some basic issues of the simulations. Simulation results in terms of welfare and output changes are then reported and analyzed. They relate to two integration scenarios: one with a 50 per cent reduction in intra-MERCOSUR tariffs and the other with a 100 per cent reduction. A comparison of the results from simulating Bertrand and Cournot firm behavior is also presented. The last section focuses on the problem of policy harmonization between MERCOSUR countries. Two central issues here are inter-country disparities in tariffs on imports from third countries and inter-country disparities in exchange policy.

5.1 Description of the Model and the Calibration Procedure

As stated earlier, the effect of integration is to be simulated within the framework of the partial equilibrium model developed by Smith and Venables (1988). Partial equilibrium in an individual industry refers to the partition of the world into a number of "countries" and the emerging pattern of production and consumption observed in 1985. The countries in this case are Argentina, Brazil, Uruguay, the rest of the LAIA (ROL), and the rest of the world (ROW). Paraguay, the least industrialized among the four MERCOSUR countries, was included in the ROL, as no industrial statistics for this country at the level of aggregation required by the present study were available.

The main differences here compared to former applications of this model are related to the structure of real trade costs that prevailed in the base year. In the cases of the studies on the EC and EFTA countries mentioned above, trade costs could be equated with transport costs or with the costs of customs formalities. Accordingly, the authors of the two studies assumed that market share differences across countries were explained by a uniform trade cost of 10 per cent in addition to consumer preferences. The authors of the study on Spain's entry into the EC, however, had to specify four additional costs, namely, Spain's pre-integration EC tariff and EC's tariff on Spanish goods, as well as Spain's and the EC's tariffs on imports from third countries. In the present case, we had to estimate a 5×5 matrix of tariff levels for each of the seven industries under study.

In the Smith-Venables model, actual data on consumption, production, and exports for an individual industry are combined with exogenous parameters to compute a number of endogenous variables and parameters. This is the process of calibration. It consists of solving the equations system derived from the demand, supply and equilibrium conditions specified by the model.

5.1.1 The Model

There are assumed to be I markets and firms located in one market or another. There are n_i identical firms in each market, which produce m_i types of a differentiated product under economies of scale and scope. The firms are able to ship to the other markets by incurring a transport cost in addition to tariffs. Accordingly, observed consumption in country j of products produced in country i can be denoted by $n_i m_i x_{ij} p_{ij}$, observed production in country i by $n_i m_i \Sigma x_{ij} p_{ij}$, and firms' net receipts by $n_i m_i \Sigma x_{ij} p_{ij}(1\text{-}t_{ij})$, where x, p, and t stand respectively for quantities, prices, and trade costs inclusive of tariffs.

As firms in each individual country are assumed to be perfectly symmetric in models and thus in quantities and prices, the analysis can be carried out in terms of one "representative firm" for each country. Here follows a short description of the model. For more details see the Methodological Appendix, and Smith and Venables (1988).

The supply side of the model is represented by the profit equation:

$$\pi_i = m_i \sum_j \left[x_{ij} p_{ij} (1 - t_{ij})\right] - C_i(x_i, m_i), \quad i=1,\dots I; \tag{5.1}$$

where C_i is the firm's production cost function. The profit function is increasing in both output per model ($x_i = \Sigma x_{ij}$) and in the number of model varieties produced (m_i). The form of the cost function is a weighted average of a linear and a log-linear function.

Demand for individual product varieties is given by

$$x_{ij} = p_{ij}^{\varepsilon} a_{ij} b_j q_j^{\varepsilon - \mu} \quad , \; i,j = 1,...I; \tag{5.2}$$

where a_{ij} is the parameters describing consumer preferences, b_j is the parameters measuring the size of the markets, ε is the elasticity of demand for a single differentiated product, and *m* the constant elasticity of demand for the entire industry. q_j is the aggregate price levels of the product in country *j*; they are derived from the sub-utility function according to the following formula:

$$q_j = \left[\sum_{ij} a_{ij} n_i m_i p_{ij}^{1-\phi} \right]^{1/(1-\varepsilon)} \tag{5.3}$$

Maximization of profit function (1) with respect to x_{ij} and m_i give first order conditions (4) and (5), respectively

$$p_{ij}\,(1\text{-}t_{ij})\,(1\text{-}1/e_{ij}) = (1/m_i)\; dC_i/dx_i, \quad i,j = 1,...I; \tag{5.4}$$

$$\sum_{ij} \left[x_{ij} p_{ij} (1 - \theta_{ij}) \right] = \partial C_i / \partial m_i \, , \; i\text{=}1,...I; \tag{5.5}$$

where e_{ij}=$e(v_i,e,m,s_{ij})$ is the perceived elasticities of demand and q_{ij}=$q(w_i,e,m,s_{ij})$ summarize the reactions of the firm when the number of models changes. s_{ij} denotes the share of a single representative firm from country *i* in country *j*. v_i is the firm's conjectures about the response of other firms to a change in output (Cournot behavior) or in prices (Bertrand behavior), and they are assumed to be zero[1]. w_i is the firm conjectures about the response of other firms to a change in the number of models they produce and they are assumed to take on non-zero values. The functional form of *e* and *q* depends on the choice of the output game: Cournot or Bertrand, as shown in the Appendix.

5.1.2 Calibration

The system of nonlinear equations represented by (5.2) to (5.5) characterizes the equilibrium of the segmented market with a fixed number of firms. A number of endogenous variables and parameters are to be calculated: quantities (*x*) and prices (*p*) by selling and buying country; levels of costs (*c*), number of models (*m*), and conjectures (*w*) by selling country; and the model elasticity (*e*). In order to close the model, additional equations need to be specified. This is done by means of the following normalizing assumptions:

The quantity produced by each representative firm is normalized to one:

---

[1] Smith and Venables set v_i=0, arguing that since product differentiation was a characteristic of the industries under study, price-cost margins may be supported by zero conjectures.

$$\sum_j x_{ij} = 1. \tag{5.6}$$

Overall profits at the LAIA level are zero:

$$\sum_{i=1...4} \pi_i = 0. \tag{5.7}$$

The number of models produced in country 1 (Argentina) is equal to observed sales

$$m_1 = \sum_j (p_{1j} x_{1j} m_1 n_1 / n_1). \tag{5.8}$$

Firms are assumed to have the same cost function in all the countries

$$C_i = C_1, \quad i=2,...I\text{-}1. \tag{5.9}$$

Note that (5.6) implies that the number of models is a proxy for firm size while (5.7) implies that equilibrium profits are in fact deviations from average LAIA profitability.

Demand parameters a_{ij} and b_j are calibrated as follows. a_{ij} is calculated as the differences between the magnitudes that Smith and Venables called tariff equivalents and real trade costs. The former are defined as the hypothetical tariff rates which would make the firm's shares of different national markets consistent with observed shares when demand functions are assumed to be uniform across markets. b_j, in turn, is calibrated to equate total sales in each market with corresponding observed values. Finally, cost function parameters are calibrated using information on the minimum efficient scale (MES), and the percentage increases in average cost at 1/2 of the MES scale.

Accordingly, calibration demanded the compilation of the following data by industry: the 5×5 matrix of sales in country i of goods produced in country j, the number of firms in each country, the elasticity of aggregate demand, the parameters of the cost function, the 5×5 matrix of tariffs, and the transport costs. The entire set of data and parameters as well as the results of calibration for all of the selected industries are displayed in the appendix table A19. Table 5.1 reports MERCOSUR averages of calibration results for all seven industries. The table also provides a summary description of each industry.

Indexes in the table include the percentage index of preferences for foreign products (ξ) and the Herfindahl index of concentration. The former has been derived from the parameters a_{ij} according to formula (5.10).

$$\xi = \frac{\sum_{j=i} a_{ij}}{\sum_j a_{ij}}. \tag{5.10}$$

Table 5.1. Calibration results, basic data, and parameters; all industries;. 1985. Million of dollars and percentages

Mercosur aggregates and averages	Synthetic fibers	Pharmaceutical products	Bricks and clay products	Office machinery	Electrical machinery	Electrical household app.	Motor vehicles
Data and parameters							
Market elasticity	0.50	0.80	0.60	0.90	1.10	1.75	1.63
Number of sub-industries	1.00	5.00	1.00	2.00	2.00	3.00	1.00
Number of firms	32.00	141.00	86.00	59.00	132.00	36.00	16.00
Average firm[a]	48.09	25.32	19.97	30.28	16.42	44.62	784.24
Domestic sales[b]	93.76	98.24	97.40	87.37	96.72	98.46	93.46
Imports[c]	5.41	4.59	1.44	12.65	9.44	0.46	1.83
Herfindahl index	0.06	0.08	0.03	0.04	0.02	0.18	0.15
ROW tariff[a]	37.00	19.00	42.00	26.00	29.00	38.00	45.00
Minimum optimal size[d]	68.63	31.51	20.25	44.90	25.46	62.76	1220.39
Economies of scale[e]	10.00	22.00	15.00	10.00	15.00	10.00	-10.00
Bertrand calibration							
Product group elasticity	8.74	4.77	5.77	9.53	6.33	9.48	6.25
Model number[a]	49.00	25.00	20.00	31.00	17.00	48.00	1039.00
Model conjectures[a]	25.31	16.82	-2.21	47.79	32.35	48.91	50.49
Preference foreign prds.[a]	55.98	1.71	35.63	52.48	32.50	45.60	42.76
Price index[a]	1.37	2.17	1.80	1.44	1.84	1.37	1.77
Profitability[f]	4.21	24.46	3.72	2.60	5.15	14.35	63.89
Gov. tariff revenue[d]	122.38	65.60	25.80	202.21	245.94	12.56	548.83
Tariff equivalents[g]	41.21	85.59	63.46	43.77	49.89	49.75	63.28

Table 5.1 (cont.). Calibration results, basic data, and parameters; all industries;. 1985. Million of dollars and percentages

Mercosur aggregates and averages	Synthetic fibers	Pharmaceutical products	Bricks and clay products	Office machinery	Electrical machinery	Electrical household app.	Motor vehicles
Cournot calibration							
Product group elasticity	23.22	6.29	6.95	12.48	6.74	19.63	8.53
Model number[a]	50.00	77.00	59.00	30.00	17.00	49.00	1056.00
Model conjectures[a]	-2.20	-1.81	-2.19	2.17	4.41	-2.71	4.26
Preference foreign prds.[a]	70.96	1.86	41.19	54.15	33.13	53.46	47.89
Price index[a]	1.22	1.79	1.66	1.34	1.74	1.19	1.46
Profitability[f]	66.55	138.28	34.99	23.88	25.35	66.33	218.39
Gov. tariff revenue[d]	122.38	65.60	25.80	202.21	245.94	12.56	548.23
Tariff equivalents[g]	31.61	78.16	58.75	38.19	48.55	36.53	54.03

[a] Unweighted average

[b] As % of production

[c] As % of apparent consumption

[d] Millions of dollars

[e] Increase in average costs at 1/2 output per model; motor vehicles: 2 output per model

[f] Unweighted average from deviations from LAIA average

[g] Intra-MERCOSUR

Note that in principle, a_{ij} would describe the propensity of consumers in country j to acquire the products from country i. In practice, however, the index computed according to (5.10) could be inconsistent with actual consumers' preferences because of the action of exogenous variables. Pharmaceutical products provide an example of this. The extremely low magnitude of the index computed for this industry does not mean that MERCOSUR consumers tend to buy domestic products, but simply that imports are constrained by extensive administrative controls.

The Herfindahl index, in turn, provides a measure of market concentration, including sales by foreign firms. Hence, the higher the index the less competitive the industry. It is evident from the formal structure of the model that variations in this index alter the elasticity of substitution and therefore the order of magnitude of welfare and output changes.

Note, finally, that elasticities resulting from Bertrand calibration are systematically lower than those resulting from Cournot calibration. This is explained by the fact that strategic interactions due to product differentiation are stronger when firms compete on prices. The smallest differences between the two elasticities are recorded for industries in which the Herfindahl index is low. Bricks and clay products and electrical machinery provide examples of this.

5.2 Sources of Data and Exogenous Parameters

Data on exports for MERCOSUR countries by industrial origin and country of destination were obtained from published national trade statistics and miscellaneous sources. The value of ROL exports to MERCOSUR countries was derived from import data provided by the same sources, after adjustments were made for differences between f.o.b. and c.i.f. prices. The value of ROL exports to the ROW was calculated by deducting MERCOSUR exports to the ROW as well as intra-LAIA trade from LAIA's overall exports. A similar procedure was used when estimating the value of ROL imports from the ROW.

Values of production expressed in national currencies were obtained from industrial censuses and annual surveys for MERCOSUR countries. These were converted to dollars by using real exchange rates, i.e., official exchange rates adjusted by changes in relative price indices around 1985. The number of representative firms in each MERCOSUR country was computed as the inverse of the Herfindhal index of concentration. The indexes were derived from census data on employment by size of establishment[2]. Some adjustments were made so that these figures corresponded to the unknown size distribution of firms[3]. Data on production and on the number of firms for both the ROL and the ROW were not

[2] They thus differ from the indices stated in the tables.

[3] Census data on the number of firms were available for Brazil but not for Argentina or Uruguay. For these two countries the adjustment was made on the data provided by miscellaneous sources.

available. Hence, we had to make some gross estimations of these magnitudes. As a norm, we estimated the value of production and the number of firms for the ROL as equal to corresponding magnitudes for the total of MERCOSUR countries[4]. We further assumed a value of production for the ROW that made the ratio of its output to its exports to LAIA-countries the same as the ratio of these countries' output to their exports. Firm size was assumed to be equal to the MERCOSUR average for both the ROL and the ROW.[5]

The computation of 1985 tariffs was rather complex. For each individual industry and MERCOSUR country, we first estimated the *ad valorem* tariff, which the country charged on its imports from the ROW. The information was provided by the statistical office of the LAIA at Montevideo, and from customs publications by each country. The estimation was made by averaging the legal *ad valorem* tariffs, which applied to the main products imported by the country in 1985. In some cases, we weighted the *ad valorem* tariffs by corresponding import values. Intra-MERCOSUR tariffs were then computed by adjusting basic ROW tariffs according to the preferential reductions stipulated by relevant agreements. Finally, we computed tariffs on trade between MERCOSUR countries and the ROL by adjusting their respective ROW tariffs according to the 10 per cent reduction granted by the LAIA agreement mentioned above[6]. As can be observed in Table 5.1, ROW tariffs are high for MERCOSUR countries. The unweighted average tariff for the selected industries is 34 per cent. Note, however, that there are considerable variations in tariff levels among industries. Inter-country differences (not displayed in the table) are also of importance. The tariffs range from a high of 39 per cent for Brazil to 19 per cent for Argentina. Uruguay's average tariff is 27 per cent.

As already mentioned, basic trade costs include transport and costs for customs formalities. These are likely to vary according to distance and membership in the integration schemes. Hence, we assumed differential trade costs by export market: 15 per cent for all trade with the ROW, 11.25 per cent for MERCOSUR trade with the ROL, and 7.5 per cent for intra-MERCOSUR trade. Six of the seven industries included in this study make up a subset of the industries considered by Smith and Venables (1988). For these industries, the market elasticity of demand and cost parameters other than the MES was taken from the mentioned study. For bricks and clay products, the seventh industry, an elasticity identical to the one used by Smith and Venables when calibrating the cement industry was assumed. Cost parameters in turn were taken from Pratten (1988). It was finally assumed that the

---

[4] The exception was motor vehicles. The ROL value of production for this industry was estimated on the basis of data on Mexico, the other large producer in the region.

[5] A similar approach was adopted by Smith and Venables (1988) and Gual, Martínez-Giralt, and Vives (1989) when estimating the same magnitudes for the ROW and for the rest of the EC. We have to remark, as these authors did, on the artificial nature of these figures and the need for caution when interpreting results for the ROL and the ROW.

[6] The ROL'S ROW tariff was estimated as the average of corresponding MERCOSUR tariffs.

average MERCOSUR firm was a proxy for the MES for all of the selected industries[7].

A final remark should be made about the division of the selected industries into a number of symmetric sub-industries. Smith and Venables justified this procedure by referring to the heterogeneous product composition of the output of statistically aggregate industries. The authors argued that this would in many cases preclude the model from capturing 'the competitive interaction between firms at a disaggregate product level'. The argument also applies to the industries selected for analysis by the present study. Note, however, that the number of sub-industries stipulated in the tables may differ from those in the Smith-Venables study due to divergencies in the definition of an individual industry.[8]

5.3 Simulating Trade Liberalization

Preferential tariff-reductions are incorporated into the model quite simply: they diminish trade costs within the MERCOSUR and the LAIA, thereby altering relative prices. The economic effects of these variations in terms of welfare and output can then be estimated by simulating various competition frameworks (Bertrand or Cournot), diverse market conditions (the number of firms is allowed to vary or not to vary), and different degrees of market integration (markets are segmented or completely integrated).[9]

Clearly, the scenario characterized by fully integrated markets is not relevant for this study. It corresponds to the objective that EC countries are presently close to achieving, that is, the integration of national markets into an economic union. By contrast, the integration process of MERCOSUR countries is in its earliest phase, namely, the building of a customs union. Consequently, the policy experiments undertaken in this study are exclusively related to an integration scenario where firms are still able to price discriminate between different national markets.

Adjustment costs produced by trade liberalization and/or economic integration are likely to be strongest for highly protected economies. Firms and workers, for instance, may be substantially injured by the elimination of trade barriers and irreparable damage may be caused to domestic production by import competition. This would be particularly true for countries carrying production at levels below the MES because of insufficient domestic market size. In such cases, the ultimate market outcome of integration for an individual country may be not only the exit of the marginal domestic firms but of all firms, with a subsequent falling off of

---

[7] Two reasons for making this assumption were the shortage of scale-efficiency measures for Latin American countries and the fact that the engineering estimates which appear in the Smith-Venables study relate to industrialised economies.

[8] This in turn depends on discrepancies between the industry classifications used in the studies: the NACE in the Smith-Venables study and the ISIC in the present one.

[9] The model also allows for simulating fixed or variable number of models.

employment and consumption levels. Actually, such negative effects are often mitigated by state interventions, by acquisition of local firms by foreign competitors or simply by direct investment by foreign firms interested in producing for the enlarged market.[10] These dynamics of the integration process are omitted from the comparative statics our simulations depict. Hence, the collapse of individual industries as forecasted by some of our policy experiments should be interpreted with caution, as being indicative of the increasing efforts to coordinate industrial and foreign investment legislation that governments should make when integration gains momentum. Subject to these qualifications, we carry out simulations that allow for both fixed and variable number of firms. For the latter case, an additional condition for equilibrium is that profits will be zero for all firms in the industry, that is,

$$\pi_i = 0, \quad i{=}i,...I.. \qquad (5.11)$$

Two standard models for dealing with imperfect competition are proposed in the literature: the Cournot and the Bertrand models, which assume quantities and prices, respectively, as the firms' strategical variables. Research has shown that the appropriateness of one model or the other for the purposes of empirical analysis cannot be decided on a priori grounds. It is rather a matter of the characteristics of the industries under study, mainly their technologies of production and their market structures. In any case, it is now the usual practice to report the results of both Cournot and Bertrand simulations. We follow this practice in the present study although we think that there is reason for presupposing that modeling competition on Bertrand assumptions fits actual firm behavior in MERCOSUR countries better.

A central argument in this connection is related to the widespread use of import quotas as protection devices by MERCOSUR countries. Bhagwati's conclusion about the lack of equivalence between tariffs and quotas raises doubts about the relevancy of Cournot assumptions in the present context. Note indeed that firms behaving according to Cournot assumptions take quantities and thus imports as given. Since quotas and tariffs do not normally lead to the same level of imports, it is unlikely that domestic firms envisaging important changes in trade policy would react according to Cournot lines. Domestic firms would most probably expect the supply shocks from abroad to be larger when the quota is eliminated than when the tariff is abolished. Moreover, with differentiated products protected by both import quotas and high tariffs, the risk for a serious loss in domestic market share can persist for local firms even when tariffs are eliminated but quotas are maintained. This is the case when domestic firms gain knowledge that consumer preferences do not allow for demanding the quantity of foreign goods specified by the quota at the pre-tariff reduction price but do so at

---

[10] These investments may be stimulated by cost advantages related to the individual country's endowments of skills, management capacity, raw materials, and energy sources as well as by its geographical location.

the post-tariff reduction price. Thus, it seems reasonable to assume that, in both situations, the domestic firm's response function is one based on prices rather than on quantities which is equivalent to adopting the Bertrand approach. Hence, we choose Bertrand behavior as our central case and then analyze the differences that emerge from assuming Cournot behavior in the simulations.

5.3.1 Reducing Trade Barriers

In this section, we discuss the results of two policy experiments that incorporate the program of tariff reductions described in section three. We first simulate a 50 per cent reduction in intra-MERCOSUR tariffs and a 50 per cent increase in LAIA preferential tariff reductions (Table 5.2), and then scale up both magnitudes to 100 per cent (Table 5.3). These scenarios correspond approximately to the extent of preferential tariff reductions that should be achieved in 1993 and 1995. respectively. Simulations are carried for both fixed and variable number of firms, assuming Bertrand behavior.[11]

Direct observation of the tables reveals a number of interesting features of simulation results:

5.3.2 Welfare Gains

Changes in welfare are defined as the sum of changes in consumer surplus, profits, and government tariff revenues. Changes in MERCOSUR aggregate welfare are in columns 4 and 8 of Tables 5.2 and 5.3. As emerges from these figures, aggregate welfare improves in all industries. A comparison of the four simulations depicted by the tables shows that the strongest differential impact is the one associated with changes in the level of tariff reduction. When the number of firms is assumed to be fixed, the average increase in aggregate welfare as per cent of consumption is 0.17 per cent, for a 50 per cent reduction in tariffs. Letting the number of firms vary does not alter this figure.

The increase in welfare notably is amplified, however, when the countries build a free trade area as in Table 5.3, augmenting up to 0.32 and 0.33 per cent on the average for fixed and variable number of firms, respectively. This is mainly due to the fact that the loss of tariff revenues tends to be compensated by larger increases in consumer surplus when trade liberalization goes further. The removal of all reciprocal tariff barriers, on the other hand, may place MERCOSUR countries in a dilemma because of the large proportion of government revenues that comes from customs duties. The dilemma is particularly serious for those industries that enjoyed high levels of tariff protection. In these cases, trade liberalization will certainly reduce price and increase consumer surplus, thus improving overall welfare. Yet, the extent of the loss of tariff revenues could

[11] The entire set of results relating to both Bertrand and Cournot assumptions will be supplied by the author on request.

Table 5.2. Reduction of trade barriers; all industries. Competition: Bertrand
Experiment: 50 % Reduction in intra-MERCOSUR tariffs and 50% increase in LAIA preferential tariff reductions

	Fixed number of firms				Variable number of firms			
	Argentina	Brazil	Uruguay	MERCOSUR	Argentina	Brazil	Uruguay	MERCOSUR
Synthetic fibers								
Δ % in production	-1.10	0.61	8.92	0.51	-1.47	0.62	11.56	0.51
Δ % in average cost	0.13	-0.07	-1.07	-0.06	-0.15	-0.03	-0.70	0.05
Δ in welfare as % consumption	0.60	0.14	0.32	0.21	0.65	0.13	0.18	0.21
Pharmaceutical products								
Δ % in production	0.03	0.04	-0.52	0.02	0.03	0.04	-0.69	0.02
Δ % in average cost	-0.01	-0.01	0.13	-0.00	-0.00	-0.00	-0.01	-0.00
Δ in welfare as % consumption	0.01	0.01	-0.06	0.01	0.01	0.02	-0.08	0.01
Bricks & clay products								
Δ % in production	-0.76	0.28	-7.40	0.15	-0.52	0.34	-57.60	0.07
Δ % in average cost	0.14	-0.05	1.39	-0.03	-0.00	-0.01	-0.71	-0.01
Δ in welfare as % consumption	-0.01	0.06	12.64	0.07	0.00	0.06	12.87	0.07
Office machinery								
Δ % in production	2.02	0.53	-6.95	0.61	23.56	0.54	-48.54	1.92
Δ % in average cost	-0.22	-0.06	0.80	-0.06	-0.05	-0.00	-0.02	-0.00
Δ in welfare as % consumption	0.02	0.07	-1.11	0.06	0.03	0.05	-0.32	0.05

Table 5.2 (cont.). Reduction of trade barriers; all industries. Competition: Bertrand
Experiment: 50 % Reduction in intra-MERCOSUR tariffs and 50% increase in LAIA preferential tariff reductions

	Fixed number of firms				Variable number of firms			
	Argentina	Brazil	Uruguay	MERCOSUR	Argentina	Brazil	Uruguay	MERCOSUR
Electrical machinery								
Δ % in production	3.37	0.09	-15.56	0.24	6.00	0.25	-100.00	0.34
Δ % in average cost	-0.53	-0.01	2.88	-0.04	-0.05	-0.00	-0.00	-0.02
Δ in welfare as % consumption	0.42	0.05	0.59	0.08	0.51	0.05	-0.10	0.09
Electrical household appliances								
Δ % in production	3.80	-0.34	-8.34	0.19	4.07	-0.32	-16.85	0.15
Δ % in average cost	-0.49	0.04	1.37	-0.01	-0.36	-0.03	-0.48	-0.08
Δ in welfare as % consumption	0.42	0.13	1.23	0.19	0.41	0.14	2.01	0.21
Motor vehicles								
Δ % in production	5.32	-0.29	-38.03	0.46	6.25	-0.31	-80.45	0.46
Δ % in average cost	-0.93	0.05	9.99	-0.08	-0.49	-0.06	-0.10	-0.14
Δ in welfare as % consumption	0.98	0.42	3.73	0.53	1.04	0.43	3.52	0.56

Table 5.3. Reduction of trade barriers; all industries. Competition: Bertrand
Experiment: 100 % reduction in intra-MERCOSUR tariffs and 100% increase in LAIA preferential tariff reductions

	Fixed number of firms				Variable number of firms			
	Argentina	Brazil	Uruguay	MERCOSUR	Argentina	Brazil	Uruguay	MERCOSUR
Synthetic fibers								
Δ % in production	3.74	0.89	23.55	1.55	3.19	0.88	33.15	1.60
Δ % in average cost	-0.44	-0.11	-2.59	-0.16	-0.57	-0.08	-1.51	-0.13
Δ in welfare as % consumption	1.02	0.21	0.71	0.33	1.02	0.21	0.47	0.32
Pharmaceutical products								
Δ % in production	0.07	0.09	-1.11	0.05	0.08	0.09	-1.49	0.05
Δ % in average cost	-0.02	-0.02	0.27	-0.01	-0.01	-0.00	-0.02	-0.01
Δ in welfare as % consumption	0.02	0.03	-0.18	0.02	0.02	0.03	-0.23	0.02
Bricks & clay products								
Δ % in production	-1.99	0.51	56.43	0.43	-1.48	0.78	-100.00	0.24
Δ % in average cost	0.36	-0.09	-7.10	-0.08	-0.01	-0.02	-0.00	-0.02
Δ in welfare as % consumption	-0.14	0.12	26.62	0.14	-0.14	0.13	15.14	0.12
Office machinery								
Δ % in production	7.72	1.05	4.19	1.46	113.48	0.45	-63.07	7.36
Δ % in average cost	-0.78	-0.12	-0.44	-0.15	-0.14	-0.01	-0.16	0.01
Δ in welfare as % consumption	0.04	0.13	-3.41	0.11	0.40	0.07	-3.53	0.08

Table 5.3 (cont.). Reduction of trade barriers; all industries. Competition: Bertrand
Experiment: 100 % reduction in intra-MERCOSUR tariffs and 100% increase in LAIA preferential tariff reductions

	Fixed number of firms				Variable number of firms			
	Argentina	Brazil	Uruguay	MERCOSUR	Argentina	Brazil	Uruguay	MERCOSUR
Electrical machinery								
Δ % in production	11.18	0.04	-26.51	0.62	19.33	0.05	-100.00	0.92
Δ % in average cost	-1.65	-0.01	5.54	-0.09	-0.15	-0.01	-0.00	-0.01
Δ in welfare as % consumption	1.24	0.05	-0.42	0.13	1.50	0.05	-0.55	0.15
Electrical household appliances								
Δ % in production	22.80	-2.62	-32.53	0.88	26.05	-2.60	-80.11	0.84
Δ % in average cost	-2.56	0.32	6.85	-0.05	-1.71	-0.08	-1.06	-0.34
Δ in welfare as % consumption	2.22	0.08	-0.57	0.42	2.29	0.13	-0.78	0.47
Motor vehicles								
Δ % in production	26.54	-2.45	-71.88	1.80	35.10	-3.98	-100.00	1.74
Δ % in average cost	-4.01	0.44	35.91	-0.24	-1.84	-0.12	-0.00	-0.26
Δ in welfare as % consumption	3.88	0.50	2.53	1.10	4.55	0.44	4.03	1.18

eventually lead to undesirable tax pressures on domestic consumption. The risk is considerably augmented when the share of intra-regional imports in consumption was large at the base year or when integration causes imports from partners to increase at the expense of imports from non-partners. Examples of this are electrical household appliances and motor vehicles, where the loss of tariff revenues due to a 100 per cent tariff cut is of about 20 per cent of base values.

The ranking of industries according to the size of aggregate welfare changes remains almost stable when we move from the 50 per cent to the 100 per cent tariff reduction scenario or when the assumption of a fixed number of firms is relaxed. The largest gains in welfare are achieved in electrical household appliances, motor vehicles and synthetic fibers. Again, the explanation is that these industries had relatively large ratios of intra-regional imports to consumption in 1985. Additionally, they have significant returns to scale. The gains, however, are very modest, even for the zero-tariff equilibrium. Welfare gains greater than 1 per cent of base consumption are observed only in the case of motor vehicles. At the national level of analysis, the magnitude of the welfare index tends to be inversely correlated with the size of the country. For the zero tariff with fixed-number-of-firms scenario, the index is 3.6, 1.2, and 0.16 on the average for Uruguay, Argentina, and Brazil, in this order. Uruguay also records the largest differences in welfare change across industries. The changes range from -3.4 per cent in office machinery to 26.6 per cent in bricks and clay products for the reference equilibrium. Welfare effects for Brazil and Argentina are positive almost throughout while they are negative for Uruguay in four of the seven industries. Evidently, these observations lend some support to the argument in favor of lengthening the transitional period for attaining a zero-tariff, for Uruguay as well as for Paraguay. Note, however, that in two cases, namely, synthetic fibers and bricks and clay products, welfare considerably improves when the reduction in tariffs is scaled up from 50 to 100 per cent.

The analysis above again raises the controversial question of the advantages and disadvantages of integrating countries, which differ widely in size and levels of industrialization. As we shall see immediately, further insight into this question is provided by the rationalization process caused by integration and by the national distribution of changes in output.

5.3.3 Changes in Output and Average Costs

As previously noted, a matter of concern for MERCOSUR countries is the extent of the inter-industry adjustment which would follow the abolition of reciprocal tariffs. Indeed, policy makers are concerned by the costs of managing this adjustment more than by some hypothetical change in national income. In addition, the desire for a higher level of industrialization or, conversely, the fear of deindustrialization, are likely to shift the subject of public concern from the extent of welfare gains to less esoteric questions. One of these is about the ability of local firms to meet foreign competition on both the domestic and the regional markets.

We approach the issue by focusing on changes in trade patterns, production, and average costs.

The first effect of a preferential trade agreement is to reduce tariff-adjusted prices of imports from members in relation to the prices of imports from outsiders. This shifts expenditures, reshapes trade flows, and affects output levels. In the present case, the tariff-adjusted prices of intra-MERCOSUR imports fall in relation to the prices of imports from both the rest of LAIA and the rest of the world. As a consequence, expenditures are shifted away from extra-MERCOSUR produced goods, thereby increasing profits for and encouraging production by MERCOSUR firms. When equilibrium is restored, the emerging trade pattern is one of expanding intra-MERCOSUR and intra-LAIA trade and, often, of contracting trade with the ROW. As shown in Table 5.4, the former effect is rather small for pharmaceutical products, moderate for bricks and clay products, office machinery, and electrical power machinery, and quite dramatic for artificial fibers, electrical household appliances, and motor vehicles. Intra-MERCOSUR trade grows by 130 and 500 per cent on the average for a 50 per cent and a 100 per cent tariff cut respectively. Evidently, a longer period of time would be needed to see how wrong these estimates might be, considering that the former level of preferential tariff reductions was to be reached by 1993 and the latter by 1995. Some evidence may, however, be provided on this issue by considering current trends in two-way trade among MERCOSUR countries. Between 1988 (the year prior to the Argentine-Brazilian agreement) and 1993, the increment in intra-MERCOSUR overall exports was 300 per cent, larger than the increment produced by the 50 per cent simulation but smaller than the increment produced by the 100 per cent simulation. Evidently, this comparison is of limited practical relevance for evaluating the accuracy of our estimates. They are based on data for seven manufacturing industries while actual figures refer to all economic sectors, including agriculture. The comparison, however, is useful in the sense that it indicates that the order of magnitude of estimated trade effects does not differ extremely from that suggested by actual growth trends.

As already stated, changes in output tend to be symmetrical to changes in the trade pattern. Tables 5.2 and 5.3 show that the removal of tariff barriers on intra-MERCOSUR trade leads to the growth of MERCOSUR output in all industries. Assuming a fixed number of firms, the average output increment is 0.3 per cent for a 50 per cent tariff reduction and 0.9 per cent for a 100 per cent tariff reduction. Larger figures are obtained when the assumption is relaxed: 0.5 per cent and 1.8 per cent, respectively. The national distribution of the production increases, however, ultimately depends on the effects of both gaining access to a broader market and greater competition from partner countries for domestic firms. The expansion of intra-MERCOSUR trade, indeed, raises competition in each market and consequently tends to produce losses in domestic shares in all markets. Overall, the dimension of these market losses (non-expelled in the tables) is inversely correlated to the size of the country. For Brazil, the loss of domestic share ranges from zero to 4.9 per cent, whereas it ranges from 1.4 to 55 per cent

Table 5.4. Changes in trade patterns. MERCOSUR aggregates. Bertrand calibration

		Fixed number of firms					Variable number of firms				
Tariff		Intra-Mercosur	Trade with ROL		Trade with ROW		Intra-Mercosur	Trade with ROL		Trade with ROW	
reduction	Reduction	Trade	Imports	Exports	Imports	Exports	Trade	Imports	Exports	Imports	Exports
Artificial	50	130.5	20.0	32.6	-2.4	0.3	133.0	20.1	32.9	-2.4	0.3
fibers	100	502.5	32.5	76.0	-7.5	0.6	509.9	30.0	78.4	-7.8	0.6
Pharmaceutical	50	24.9	9.4	6.5	-0.1	0.0	25.3	9.4	6.5	-0.1	0.0
products	100	55.0	19.5	13.2	-0.2	0.0	56.0	19.4	13.2	-0.2	0.0
Bricks & clay	50	102.8	10.0	25.6	-0.4	-0.1	85.7	13.1	25.4	-0.2	-3.5
products	100	296.1	26.3	56.8	-1.0	1.7	172.6	27.7	56.3	-0.5	-5.8
Office	50	59.2	7.5	20.5	-1.8	0.2	58.5	3.2	28.4	-3.4	8.4
machinery	100	162.3	15.0	45.0	-4.2	0.8	186.4	-2.8	87.7	-10.2	38.6
Electrical	50	74.8	19.7	15.8	-0.6	0.1	70.6	18.8	16.4	-1.1	0.3
machinery	100	212.1	42.5	33.8	-1.5	0.2	219.9	39.3	36.1	-3.1	1.4
Electrical	50	262.3	19.5	38.7	-5.0	-0.1	269.2	20.7	38.8	-2.1	-0.3
household	100	1263.3	34.2	90.0	-14.7	-1.1	1410.3	34.7	89.6	-8.1	-2.2
Motor	50	253.8	45.7	31.9	-2.6	-0.1	273.5	43.3	32.7	-3.0	-0.5
vehicles	100	1006.9	105.8	71.6	-8.3	-0.7	1148.9	97.9	72.3	-12.4	-3.6

for Uruguay and from 0.1 to 12.5 for Argentina. This suggests that integration would reinforce market power for firms located in Brazil. The main factor behind this is the high likelihood for Argentine and Uruguay firms to incur inefficiency costs in the form of suboptimal production scale. As shown in *Chapter 2*, the Brazilian market is large enough to reach MES for most products while the converse is true for both Argentina and Uruguay. [12]

Integration, however, provides new trade opportunities and this may mitigate the detrimental effect of insufficient market size on the competitiveness of Argentine and Uruguayan firms. Additionally, there is the fact that trade liberalization has a differential impact on the position of firms on the domestic market because of inter-country differences in pre-integration tariffs. In fact, the higher the tariff, the larger the reduction in domestic market price and thus the greater the drop in marginal cost price. Accordingly, the relative cost disadvantage of Argentine and Uruguayan firms may be partially offset by stronger price shocks on the Brazilian market.[13]

The final outcome of these factors in terms of output changes and associated changes in average costs is given in Tables 5.2 and 5.3. Note that without adjustment in the number of firms, average costs and output necessarily move in opposite directions. This is a consequence of the assumption of decreasing marginal costs. When the number of firms is allowed to vary, a fall in production can be accompanied by a fall in average costs. This is the case when many firms exit, thus reducing aggregate output, but at the same time, remaining firms are able to expand production and to reap unexploited economies of scale.

Major output reductions are recorded for Uruguay. This, of course, is a consequence of the fact that most of Uruguay's industries operate at sub-optimal levels of production. The decline in production is sharpest when tariffs are completely removed and firms are allowed free entry and exit. For bricks and clay products, electrical machinery, electrical household appliances, and motor vehicles, the output shock is dramatic, leading to the virtual collapse of these industries. These extreme effects should be considered with caution, however. The cut in production, for instance, is significantly reduced when the number of firms is not allowed to vary. In two cases, namely bricks and clay products and office machinery, the output-cut reverts to a considerable increase. As discussed previously, what the results really suggest is that the rationalization process, taking place during the transitional period will be particularly painful for Uruguayan firms. It should be mentioned here that no specific provisions are included in the MERCOSUR agreement to facilitate such rationalization. It seems evident, however, that government intervention, foreign investment, merges, and acquisition are of crucial importance for the survival of Uruguay's industry.

---

[12] Even when the MES are approached from engineering' estimates.

[13] Inter-country differences in the costs of labour, raw material and electric power may also mitigate the effect of trade liberalization. See UNIDO (1993) for an analysis of the potential impact of these cost differentials on intra-MERCOSUR firm competition.

Competition on the enlarged market will be mainly dominated by interactions between Argentine and Brazilian firms. A general observation, which can be made from the tables, concerns the quite limited effect of the MERCOSUR trade-liberalization program on Brazilian industrial activity. Note indeed that the output shock is greater than 1 per cent only in electrical household appliances and in motor vehicles. Compare this with Argentina's large output increments in the four metal-mechanical industries. Two basic explanatory factors here are the comparatively large size of the Brazilian market[14] and the fact that the share of intra-regional trade in consumption is considerably larger for Argentina than for Brazil. Differences in the impact of tariff reductions between the two countries are quite apparent in electrical machinery, electrical household appliances and motor vehicles. Concerning electrical household appliances, a 100 per cent reduction in tariffs increases output by 23 per cent and reduces average costs by 3 per cent for Argentina. Conversely, output falls by 3 per cent and average costs rise by 0.3 per cent for Brazil. These results correspond to the assumption of a fixed number of firms. Note that average costs tend to fall for Brazil and increase for Argentina when the assumption is relaxed. This is explained by the differential impact of trade liberalization on industry rationalization, namely, a growing number of firms in Argentina and a decreasing number of firms in Brazil.

Two additional observations in terms of winners and losers can be made on the right-hand panel in Table 5.3. The industries that do best in terms of output growth are office machinery for Argentina and artificial and synthetic fibers for Brazil. The main reason for the notable competitive performance of Argentine firms in office machinery is Brazil's considerably higher tariff-level at the base year. There is also the fact that size-associated cost differentials for this industry are relatively low. These two factors enable Argentine firms to increase their share in both the domestic and the Brazilian markets when tariffs are removed. Actually, domestic market loss is relatively unimportant for Brazilian firms, amounting to less than 1 per cent. Note, however, that this represents more than 10 per cent of the Argentina market. The converse situation is true for the case of artificial and synthetic fibers. The reasons for this include weaker differences in pre-integration tariffs and the extremely small size of Argentine firms. This places the latter in a less favorable position when tariffs are removed. As a consequence, Brazil gains considerably on the Argentine and Uruguayan import markets. This largely offsets the decline in sales in its own market.

5.3.4 Bertrand *versus* Cournot

As stated earlier, there is reason to believe that the Bertrand assumptions adapt better to actual market conditions in MERCOSUR countries than do the Cournot assumptions. The arguments relate to factors not taken into account by the model, mainly quotas and administrative controls, but which still have a strong impact on

---

[14] More than five times the size of the Argentine market for the selected industries.

the market perception of firms as well as on the configuration of trade flows. There is no a prior reasoning, however, that is strong enough to assure the adequacy of one or the other hypothesis. Thus, it seems convenient to undertake a sensitivity analysis with respect to changes in market behavior assumptions.

As for the calibration results, Table 5.1 shows that the main differences are related to group elasticities and model conjectures. For the reasons stated in Section 4, product-group elasticities are systematically greater for Cournot than for Bertrand calibration, and this implies a higher degree of product differentiation in the latter case. Model conjectures are in turn significantly larger than zero for Bertrand calibration in almost all industries. Formally, this would indicate that when we assume Bertrand behavior, we are tacitly ascribing a collusive reaction-function to the firms concerning changes in the number of models. Cournot calibrations instead produce close-to-zero conjectures overall, and often they are negative; this indicates a fairly competitive equilibrium. Note, however, that as the number of models is relatively insensitive to the type of competition in the calibrations, and is assumed to be fixed in the simulations, the dilemma is more apparent than real.

Comparisons of Tables 5.2 and 5.5, alternatively 5.3 and 5.6, reveal the extent of variations in simulation results when market behavior assumptions are altered. The effects of a 50 per cent tariff reduction on MERCOSUR output are invariably enlarged when Bertrand behavior is replaced by Cournot. The reason is that the impact on prices of a tariff reduction is stronger with Cournot than with Bertrand behavior. Consequently, the increase in demand and therefore the increase in output are also greater in the former case. In terms of the MERCOSUR as a whole and in the case of a fixed number of firms, the differential effects seem relatively low, reaching a maximum of 8 percentage points in synthetic fibers. The allocation of output changes by individual country, however, is highly affected, in many cases to a extent greater than is plausible. In synthetic fibers, for instance, Argentine output falls by 1 per cent under Bertrand assumptions and increases by near 200 per cent under Cournot assumptions. Corresponding figures for Brazil are 0.6 and -18 per cent and 9 and 74 per cent for Uruguay. The differential effects are considerably enlarged when the tariff reduction is 100 per cent. With Cournot behavior, the model collapses for synthetic fibers even under the assumption of a fixed number of firms. Quite far-fetched forecasts are also obtained in the case of electrical household appliances and motor vehicles for both Argentina and Brazil, and in office machinery for Uruguay.

5.4 Customs Union and Foreign Exchange Policy

Until now, we have assumed that MERCOSUR's ROW tariffs remain unchanged. In this section, we allow these tariffs to converge into one common tariff. This, together with the removal of all intra-MERCOSUR tariff barriers corresponds to the establishment of a customs union as envisaged in the Treaty of

Table 5.5. Reduction of trade barriers: All industries. Competition: Cournot
Experiment: 50 % Reduction in intra-mercosur tariffs and 50% . Increase in LAIA preferential tariff reductions

	Fixed number of firms				Variable number of firms			
	Argentina	Brazil	Uruguay	MERCOSUR	Argentina	Brazil	Uruguay	MERCOSUR
Synthetic fibers								
Δ % in production	196.63	-18.37	73.84	8.64	409.50	-43.87	-100.00	10.16
Δ % in average cost	-13.49	3.00	-12.18	-1.44	-14.91	-0.34	-0.00	-6.25
Δ in welfare as % consumption	4.40	0.55	-2.34	1.04	5.90	7.14	4.52	6.93
Pharmaceutical products								
Δ % in production	0.06	0.06	-0.42	0.05	0.06	0.07	-0.98	0.04
Δ % in average cost	-0.01	-0.01	0.14	-0.01	-0.03	-0.01	-0.05	-0.02
Δ in welfare as % consumption	0.00	0.01	-0.12	0.01	0.01	0.01	-0.07	0.01
Bricks & clay products								
Δ % in production	-1.02	0.32	18.25	0.24	-0.67	0.48	-73.76	0.13
Δ % in average cost	0.17	-0.06	-2.93	-0.05	-0.02	-0.06	-5.53	-0.06
D in welfare as % consumption	-0.02	0.07	11.66	0.07	0.02	0.06	14.01	0.08
Office machinery								
Δ % in production	4.41	0.70	-1.72	0.93	22.95	0.69	-49.94	2.04
Δ % in average cost	-0.45	-0.08	0.19	-0.11	-0.37	-0.05	-0.54	-0.09
Δ in welfare as % consumption	-0.04	0.07	-1.64	0.05	-0.17	0.05	-0.53	0.03

Table 5.5 (cont.). Reduction of trade barriers: All industries. Competition: Cournot

Experiment: 50 % Reduction in intra-mercosur tariffs and 50% increase in LAIA preferential tariff reductions

	Fixed number of firms				Variable number of firms			
	Argentina	Brazil	Uruguay	MERCOSUR	Argentina	Brazil	Uruguay	MERCOSUR
Electrical machinery								
Δ % in production	3.88	0.09	-14.79	0.27	6.43	0.25	-100.00	0.36
Δ % in average cost	-0.65	-0.01	2.70	-0.04	-0.28	-0.01	-0.00	-0.04
Δ in welfare as % consumption	0.44	0.05	0.37	0.08	0.45	0.05	-0.02	0.08
Electrical household appliances								
Δ % in production	41.58	-5.88	-6.90	1.07	50.31	-7.60	-70.09	0.23
Δ % in average cost	-5.47	0.84	1.80	-0.00	-6.23	-0.18	-1.97	-1.11
Δ in welfare as % consumption	2.22	0.57	0.42	0.83	2.64	1.30	8.09	1.61
Motor vehicles								
Δ % in production	12.89	-1.04	-44.02	0.94	14.48	-1.50	-100.00	0.62
Δ % in average cost	-2.37	0.19	13.27	-0.13	-2.23	-0.20	-0.00	-0.48
Δ in welfare as % consumption	1.47	0.60	3.42	0.77	1.45	0.75	6.45	0.90

Table 5.6. Reduction of trade barriers: All industries. Competition: Cournot
Experiment: 100 % Reduction in intra-mercosur tariffs and 100% increase in LAIA preferential tariff reductions

	Fixed number of firms				Variable number of firms			
	Argentina	Brazil	Uruguay	MERCOSUR	Argentina	Brazil	Uruguay	MERCOSUR
Synthetic fibers								
Δ % in production	n.a	n.a	n.a	n.a	n.a	n.a	n.a	n.a
Δ % in average cost	n.a	n.a	n.a	n.a	n.a	n.a	n.a	n.a
Δ in welfare as % consumption	n.a	n.a	n.a	n.a	n.a	n.a	n.a	n.a
Pharmaceutical products								
Δ % in production	0.15	0.14	-0.90	0.12	0.14	0.15	-2.20	0.09
Δ % in average cost	-0.04	-0.03	0.30	-0.03	-0.05	-0.03	-0.12	-0.04
Δ in welfare as % consumption	0.01	0.03	-0.35	0.01	0.01	0.03	-0.24	0.02
Bricks & clay products								
Δ % in production	-2.91	0.33	255.90	0.79	-2.20	1.10	-100.00	0.44
Δ % in average cost	0.50	-0.07	-17.29	-0.20	-0.05	-0.15	-0.00	-0.13
Δ in welfare as % consumption	-0.23	0.10	38.14	0.12	-0.14	0.13	16.67	0.13
Office machinery								
Δ % in production	20.73	1.12	109.62	2.44	179.33	-1.47	732.06	10.46
Δ % in average cost	-1.86	-0.13	-6.35	-0.26	-1.35	-0.09	-4.01	-0.31
Δ in welfare as % consumption	0.15	0.07	-4.08	0.06	-0.05	0.05	-5.69	0.02

Table 5.6 (cont.). Reduction of Trade Barriers: All Industries. Competition: Cournot

Experiment: 100 % Reduction in intra-MERCOSUR tariffs and 100% Increase in LAIA preferential tariff reductions

	Fixed number of firms				Variable number of firms			
	Argentina	Brazil	Uruguay	MERCOSUR	Argentina	Brazil	Uruguay	MERCOSUR
Electrical machinery								
Δ % in production	13.48	0.01	-25.60	0.72	21.85	-0.02	-100.00	0.99
Δ % in average cost	-2.09	-0.00	5.26	-0.11	-0.84	-0.02	-0.00	-0.05
Δ in welfare as % consumption	1.34	0.04	-0.83	0.13	1.38	0.05	-0.73	0.14
Electrical household appliances								
Δ % in production	436.24	-68.09	-2.42	6.51	n.a	n.a	n.a	n.a
Δ % in average cost	-18.94	22.82	0.60	-3.64	n.a	n.a	n.a	n.a
Δ in welfare as % consumption	39.59	-2.11	-0.92	4.65	n.a	n.a	n.a	n.a
Motor vehicles								
Δ % in production	96.36	-10.97	-91.03	5.01	170.90	-26.47	-100.00	3.14
Δ % in average cost	-11.07	2.17	129.74	-0.75	-9.84	-0.39	-0.00	-2.46
Δ in welfare as % consumption	9.32	0.04	1.72	1.68	11.50	0.50	7.26	2.47

Asuncion. The issue is incorporated in the simulations by setting intra-MERCOSUR tariffs at zero and replacing base ROW tariffs with their average. The latter procedure may in part be justified by the fact that MERCOSUR countries have not yet arrived at a decision concerning the level of the common tariff. It is worth noting here that the four countries have defined a timetable for the gradual reduction of their ROW tariffs during the transitional period. However, large inter-country differences in both average tariffs and degrees of tariff dispersion make the harmonization of import policies very difficult.[15]

The efforts of MERCOSUR countries to create fair rules of competition on the common market are currently being eroded by strong fluctuations in real exchange rates. Ultimately, this may preclude the establishment of a customs union. At present, this risk is considerable. Rates of inflation and monetary conditions in MERCOSUR countries continue to diverge; meanwhile no policy coordination on the foreign exchange market has been achieved. Brazil's monthly rate of inflation was three times that of Uruguay and 10 times that of Argentina in 1992. In April of the same year, the exchange rate/inflation gap computed over 12 months was -24 percentage points for Argentina, 137 points for Brazil, and -25 points for Uruguay. All figures indicate that divergencies in real exchange rates among MERCOSUR countries will be amplified. This certainly will have a great impact on relative prices and therefore on trade flows.[16] It could thus be of interest to evaluate the welfare and production effects of variations in exchange rate parities. The scenario is the same as that described by Table 5.3, i.e., tariff-free imports from partners and differential tariffs on imports from the ROW. In accordance with observed trends, we make the following assumptions about movements in real exchange rates: Argentina currency appreciates by 5 per cent in relation to Brazil currency and by 3.75 per cent in relation to Uruguay currency in real terms. Accordingly, the Uruguay peso appreciates by 1.25 per cent in relation to the Brazil cruzado. These movements in exchange rate parities, which seem quite modest compared with past variations, are incorporated into the simulation indirectly, as changes in trade costs. These increase for Argentine shipments to Brazil and decrease for Brazilian sales to this country. Uruguay's trade costs are also altered, though to a lesser degree. Simulations were performed for both a fixed and variable number of firms. The results are displayed in Tables 5.7 and 5.8. They will be compared with those analyzed in previous sections.

---

[15] A several-tier tariff system was being negotiated at the time we performed the simulations. There were indications that the average tariff resulting from this system was to be about 30 per cent, that is, very close to the average of the basic ROW tariffs which appear in Table 5.1. As stated in the text, the four MERCOSUR countries finally agreed to set a maximum external tariff of 20 per cent.

[16] A comparison of the evolution of prices in Argentina and Brazil with the evolution of prices in the US is provided in UNIDO (1993). The results show that Argentina/Brazil's relative prices fluctuate considerably in over a 14-month period.

5.4.1 The Effects of a Common Tariff

There are marked differences in the impact of a common tariff among countries. The most striking result in the tables, however, is the sharp decrease in Brazilian output. With a variable number of firms (Table 5.8), the adjustment leads to a literal wiping out of the Brazilian office machinery industry. Serious cutbacks in production are also recorded in the other metal-mechanical industries. A crucial factor here is the increased competition of ROW firms in the Brazilian market. Indeed, a common tariff equal to MERCOSUR average duties would imply considerably lower trade barriers against ROW suppliers for Brazil. This in turn would reduce the pre-union prices of imports from ROW. Prices fall by 14 per cent on the average, causing domestic demand to shift away from home-produced products with subsequent drops in production. Increased exports to partners are not large enough to compensate local firms for the loss in domestic market share. Argentine firms in turn reap considerable gains from joining Brazil in a customs union. They increase output in all industries and achieve significant reductions in average costs. The reason here is that the common tariff raises the prices of ROW imports while as Argentine firms are still able to gain market shares in Brazil. In general, the effects are also negative for Uruguay. Exceptions include electrical household appliances and synthetic fibers. As emerges from the comparison of Tables 5.3 and 5.8, the formation of a customs union makes the rationalization process less severe in the former industry and reinforces the favorable impact of the free-trade-area in the latter. It should be recognized that these results are subject to reservations more serious than those made in the previous section. The reason is the existence of considerable nontariff barriers to trade with the ROW. These are likely to bias the pattern of price changes foreseen by the model from actual changes. This is true even when ROW tariffs remain unchanged in the simulations, but the risk undoubtedly increases when tariffs on both intra-MERCOSUR trade and trade with the ROW are allowed to vary. Note further that initial tariffs and the volume of trade affected by tariff cuts are considerably larger for the former type of trade than for the latter. It should also be noted that investment flows (including firm merging and acquisition) are likely to increase as integration gains momentum and this may reverse the effects produced by the simulations. All these factors make the results of comparative statics uncertain, especially when compared with the long-term effects on relative prices of the dismantling of nontariff barriers. This is particularly true for Brazil, where the dynamic effects of the liberalization of trade with the ROW are expected to be strongest. However, we still believe that the analysis above throws some light on the problems which Brazilian firms would encounter if a low common tariff is adopted. It further aids in understanding why Brazil is actually pressing for the common tariff to be as high as possible in several industries while other countries are hoping for a lower level. Office machinery and motor vehicles are notorious examples of this conflict.

5.4.2 The Effects of Disparities in Exchange Rate

Disparities in exchange rates (DER) considerably improve the competitive position of Brazilian firms *vis-à-vis* the Argentine ones. The effect is remarkably strong in synthetic fibers and office machinery. In the latter industry, the appreciation of Argentine peso reverses Argentine trade flows with partners radically. When free entry and exit is allowed, the switch in domestic demand forces out all local firms. In synthetic fibers, 50 per cent of the firms exit the market, and this reduces output by 40 per cent. Brazil gets most of these market shares although Uruguay and the ROL as well make some gains in the Argentine import market.

These two cases are conspicuous examples of the harmful effect that the lack of policy coordination may have on the conditions of competition. This, however, is only one part of the story. With a fixed number of firms (Table 5.7), Argentine output declines in all industries. The differential impact of DER in this case ranges from -2 per cent in pharmaceutical products to -25 per cent in electrical machinery. The comparison also allows for drawing conclusions about the differential impact of DER on average costs when the number of firms is allowed to vary. As shown in Table 5.3, these tend to fall in both Argentina and Brazil. The trend is maintained in Table 5.8, but the pattern of change in average costs is altered. Analysis of the rationalization process in motor vehicles throws light on the issue. With unchanged parities (Table 5.3), integration reduces the number of firms by 5 per cent in Brazil and increases it by 22 per cent in Argentina.[17] Output changes are in accordance with this pattern, but larger, -4 and 35 per cent, respectively. As a consequence, average costs shrunk by 0.1 per cent in Brazil and by 1.8 per cent in Argentina. When the DER are enlarged as in Table 5.8, the number of firms increases by 6 per cent in Argentina and by 2 per cent in Brazil. Corresponding output increments are 14 and 3.7 per cent. It follows that the fall in average costs will tend to be amplified in Brazil and to contract in Argentina. The percentage changes are 1.3 and 0.3 per cent, respectively.

Note, finally, that the cuts in production do not translate into such large losses in welfare due to substantial increases in both consumer surplus and tariff revenues.

5.5 Concluding Remarks

Some words of caution on the limitations of the present study are necessary before summarizing its main results. First, no general conclusion about the overall impact of integration on regional manufacturing output and welfare may be drawn from the simulations because of both the partial equilibrium nature of the model

---

[17] Changes in the number of firms are not displayed in the table. As already explained, the magnitude of these changes is endogenously determined in the simulations by assuming that profits are restored to zero for all firms in the industry (cf. equation (11) in the text).

Table 5.7. Reduction of trade barriers. All industries. Fixed number of firms (Competition: Bertrand)

Experiment: 100% Reduction in intra-MERCOSUR tariffs and 100% increase in LAIA preferential tariff reductions.

	Impact of a common external tariff				Impact of disparities in exchange rates			
	Argentina	Brazil	Uruguay	MERCOSUR	Argentina	Brazil	Uruguay	MERCOSUR
Synthetic fibers								
Δ % in production	16.18	-40.54	33.77	-32.50	-12.84	3.32	32.33	1.72
Δ % in average cost	-1.76	7.20	-3.49	5.35	1.73	- 0.39	-3.38	-0.25
Δ in welfare as % consumption	-1.95	13.96	-3.21	11.50	0.43	0.36	1.19	0.38
Pharmaceutical products								
Δ % in production	3.73	-3.41	-2.92	-1.39	-0.11	0.16	-0.82	0.06
Δ % in average cost	-0.82	0.79	0.73	0.31	0.03	-0.03	0.19	-0.01
Δ in welfare as % consumption	0.07	0.37	-0.05	0.27	0.01	0.04	-0.19	0.03
Bricks & clay products								
Δ % in production	10.32	-9.34	50.93	-7.14	-3.14	0.68	50.00	0.44
Δ % in average cost	-1.69	1.80	-6.59	1.34	0.57	-0.12	-6.49	-0.08
Δ in welfare as % consumption	-2.66	3.57	25.13	2.90	-0.16	0.15	26.24	0.15
Office machinery								
Δ % in production	47.00	-58.82	4.20	-52.23	1.93	1.98	1.62	1.98
Δ % in average cost	-3.59	14.13	-0.44	10.80	-0.20	-0.21	-0.18	-0.21
Δ in *welfare as % consumption*	-10.45	18.52	-5.05	16.27	-0.03	0.21	-3.45	0.17

Table 5.7 (cont.). Reduction of trade barriers. All industries. Fixed number of firms (Competition: Bertrand)
Experiment: 100% Reduction in intra-MERCOSUR tariffs and 100% increase in LAIA preferential tariff reductions.

	Impact of a common external tariff				Impact of disparities in exchange rates			
	Argentina	Brazil	Uruguay	MERCOSUR	Argentina	Brazil	Uruguay	MERCOSUR
Electrical machinery								
Δ % *in production*	29.86	-19.58	-32.99	-16.75	5.85	0.36	-28.87	0.60
Δ % in average cost	-3.84	3.83	7.46	3.23	-0.91	-0.06	6.20	-0.09
Δ in welfare as % consumption	-2.09	5.30	-1.86	4.75	0.79	0.07	-0.90	0.12
Electrical household appliances								
Δ % in production	20.68	-27.22	-25.09	-19.95	10.98	-0.72	-24.61	0.77
Δ % in average cost	-2.35	4.20	4.86	3.10	-1.33	0.09	4.74	-0.07
Δ in welfare as % consumption	1.58	10.12	-2.13	8.57	1.22	0.11	0.31	0.29
Motor vehicles								
Δ % in production	26.43	-30.58	-66.68	-21.92	15.49	-0.63	-70.65	1.64
Δ % in average cost	-3.99	7.30	28.96	4.96	-2.52	0.11	34.04	-0.26
Δ *in welfare as % consumption*	0.88	16.39	-0.24	13.58	2.67	0.55	2.95	0.94

Table 5.8. Reduction of trade barriers: All industries. Variable number of firms. Competition: Bertrand

Experiment: 100% Reduction in intra-MERCOSUR tariffs and 100% Increase in LAIA Preferential tariff reductions

	Impact of a common external tariff				Impact of disparities in exchange rates			
	Argentina	Brazil	Uruguay	MERCOSUR	Argentina	Brazil	Uruguay	MERCOSUR
Synthetic fibres								
Δ % *in production*	29.15	-54.90	66.84	-42.83	-40.71	11.91	68.39	6.17
Δ % in average cost	-0.57	-0.09	-1.52	0.45	-0.27	-0.17	-1.89	0.35
Δ in welfare as % consumption	-1.65	18.19	-2.81	15.13	2.94	-1.42	-0.03	-0.79
Pharmaceutical products								
Δ % in production	3.96	-3.72	-4.02	-1.57	-1.58	1.42	0.62	0.55
Δ % in average cost	-0.01	-0.00	-0.02	-0.00	-0.00	-0.02	-0.04	-0.01
Δ in welfare as % consumption	0.21	0.26	-0.17	0.23	0.06	-0.13	-0.44	-0.08
Bricks & clay products								
Δ % in production	n.a	n.a	n.a	n.a	-6.55	2.27	-100.00	1.05
Δ % in average cost	n.a	n.a	n.a	n.a	0.00	-0.04	-0.00	-0.04
Δ in welfare as % consumption	n.a	n.a	n.a	n.a	0.87	-0.07	16.03	0.06
Office machinery								
Δ % in production	439.80	-100.00	-100.00	-66.71	-100.00	14.37	97.35	7.39
Δ % in average cost	-0.09	-0.00	-0.00	0.57	-0.00	-0.05	-0.17	-0.09
Δ in welfare as % consumption	-6.50	27.30	-5.43	24.66	3.41	-2.27	-6.86	-1.86

Table 5.8 (cont.). Reduction of trade barriers: All industries. Variable number of firms. Competition: Bertrand

Experiment: 100% Reduction in intra-MERCOSUR tariffs and 100% increase in LAIA preferential tariff reductions

	Impact of a common external tariff				Impact of disparities in exchange rates			
	Argentina	Brazil	Uruguay	MERCOSUR	Argentina	Brazil	Uruguay	MERCOSUR
Electrical machinery								
Δ % in production	48.76	-27.76	-100.00	-23.52	-5.98	6.35	-100.00	5.38
Δ % in average cost	-0.16	-0.00	-0.00	0.14	-0.10	-0.01	-0.00	-0.06
Δ in welfare as % consumption	-0.94	5.95	-2.79	5.43	2.68	-1.45	-2.29	-1.16
Electrical household appliances								
Δ % in production	27.62	-33.74	-46.97	-24.61	11.60	0.97	-71.02	1.75
Δ % in average cost	-1.71	-0.09	-1.04	0.03	-0.99	-0.15	-2.07	-0.35
Δ in welfare as % consumption	2.00	11.69	-2.70	9.93	1.36	0.04	-0.92	0.24
Motor vehicles								
Δ % in production	46.02	-49.51	-100.00	-34.96	14.02	3.73	-100.00	5.00
Δ % in average cost	-1.86	-0.12	-0.00	0.32	-1.28	-0.28	-0.00	-0.45
Δ in welfare as % consumption	2.99	19.26	-7.34	16.26	3.62	-0.13	4.33	0.56

and the rather small number of sampled industries. Second, even if the model incorporates some dynamic aspects such as economies of scale and changes in market concentration, the policy experiments performed in this paper are basically exercises in comparative statics. Third, our approach has not considered the relationship between integration and flows of direct investment, including firm merging and acquisition. As the European experience demonstrates, the progressive integration of national markets tends to increase these flows and this considerably affects both trade patterns and output levels. For these reasons, our results should be at best viewed as crude approximations of the long-run effects of economic integration on trade, output, and welfare, and to the adjustment process caused by intra-regional trade liberalization.

The findings of the experiments suggest that trade among MERCOSUR countries would dramatically increase if reciprocal tariff barriers are partially or completely abolished. The rapid growth of intra-regional trade, which followed the first round of tariff reductions achieved in 1990-1992, seems to confirm these expectations. Likewise, trade with the rest of the LAIA would expand when corresponding preferential tariff reductions are augmented, though not to such large degrees. As concerns trade with the rest of world, our results indicate that imports will contract as the liberalization of intra-regional trade gains momentum. Exports in turn will increase in all but two industries, namely, electrical household appliances and motor vehicles.

In terms of output impacts and the adjustment process, the main results of the paper can be summarized as follows. Major production cutbacks and the largest adjustment costs are predicted for Uruguay. The main factor behind this is quite undersized domestic firms. On the whole, the results for Uruguay demonstrate the importance of government intervention and foreign investment for the survival of several industrial sectors. The impact of trade liberalization on economic activity is stronger for Argentina than for Brazil in relative terms. This is mainly due to the comparatively large size of Brazil's domestic market and the low weight of intra-regional trade in Brazil's consumption. In general, the results indicate that integration would reinforce market power for firms located in Brazil, notwithstanding the fact that pre-integration tariffs are considerably higher for Brazil than for Argentina. The reason again is the higher likelihood for Argentine firms to incur inefficiency costs in the form of suboptimal production scale. In cases where tariff differentials are high and size-associated cost differentials low, however, Argentine firms are able to increase output and make gains in both the domestic and the Brazilian markets.

Overall welfare gains have been computed as changes in the sum of consumer welfare, profits, and government tariff revenues. As concerns the MERCOSUR as a whole, the loss of tariff revenues tends to be matched by increases in consumer surplus. As a consequence, welfare gains are not quantitatively significant, amounting to 0.3 per cent on average. More relevant policy implications are drawn from the allocation of these gains by country. For the most part the welfare effects for Brazil and Argentina are positive, tending to increase when the tariff cut is also increased. This evidently argues in favor of accelerating the process of dismantling tariffs between the two countries. In the case of Uruguay, where the welfare effects are negative in four of the seven industries, the results instead lend some support to the argument in favor of lengthening the transitional period for attaining a zero tariff.

According to our results, current disparities in trade policies among MERCOSUR countries may create serious obstacles to the achievement of their integration objectives. A key concern here is the potential effects of adopting a low average common tariff when inter-country differences in both average tariffs and degrees of tariff dispersion are large. As shown by the experiment undertaken in this study, this is a potentially highly conflicting aspect of the integration process. Even if our quantification of the effects of forming a customs union are subject to serious reservations, it is still indicative of the importance of the issue and consistent with the experience of tariff negotiation so far. In particular, the results depict the problems which Brazilian firms would encounter if a low common tariff is adopted.

A last important result refers to the detrimental effect of disparities in exchange rates on the conditions of competition. The policy experiment undertaken in this study reveal that the output impact of the simple abolition of tariffs may be considerably altered when regional parities are moderately amplified. In the experiment, a 5 per cent appreciation of the Argentine currency *vis-à-vis* Brazil's reduces Argentine post-integration output by 2 to 25 percent.

6 Economic Integration and Economic Divergence

As it is evident from the previous chapter, discrepancies in the movement of real exchange rates can undermine the efforts of MERCOSUR countries for achieving the objective of a customs union. This evidently makes out a strong case for the harmonization of related policies. A more difficult question is whether convergence of economic performance, meaning a narrowing of disparities in growth rates and/or income levels over time, can in itself promote integration and, if so, whether it can be facilitated by coordination of macroeconomic policies. There is no such thing as a simple answer to this question. Students of the European experience, for example, have repeatedly referred to the circularity of the debate about the relationship between convergence of economic performance and integration. They point to the fact that divergence is a general and permanent feature of all complex economic systems and it should not necessarily be perceived as a bad thing in all instances (cf. Hodges and Wallace, 1981). Hence, there is no reason to equate integration with attaining homogeneity and neither to judge economic divergence as something negative in itself. Really, what is relevant is to define criteria for managing divergence rather than for eliminating it. In this chapter, we examine some aspects of this discussion in relation to the experiences of the MERCOSUR and Andean Group (GRAN) countries. We furthermore look at recent proposal to fuse these two trade blocs into a South American Free Trade Area (SAFTA). The focus is on the degree of economic interdependence between South American countries and the level of economic divergence within the region. Three specific issues are addressed, namely inter-country disparities in monetary conditions, discrepancies in the timing and design of stabilization policies, and differences in macroeconomic performance. Previously, the advance made by Latin American countries in the 1990s in both overall trade liberalization and economic integration are reviewed.

6.1 Overall Trade Liberalization as a New Integration Framework

In recent years, a large number of preferential trade agreements among individual countries or groups of countries have been signed which perhaps may be contributing to the convergence of integration efforts, but are certainly introducing further complexities into the overall process, such as double membership and group overlapping. Examples of this are the formation of the North American Free Trade Area (NAFTA), linking Mexico, which is member of the LAIA to the United States and Canada; the Group of Three agreement, which includes Mexico and two GRAN countries, namely, Venezuela and Colombia; and the agreements between individual LAIA countries and the members of the CACM and the Caribbean Community (CARICOM). Integration agreements have also proliferated in the southern part of the continent, challenging existing integration structures and institutions. There is, for instance, a formal request from Bolivia, which is a member of the GRAN, seeking membership in MERCOSUR. Additional examples are the recent four-plus-one free trade agreement between Chile and MERCOSUR, the trade agreements between Chile and individual GRAN countries, and the bilateral agreements between individual MERCOSUR and GRAN countries.

Undoubtedly, one important factor behind these advances in integration has been the current economic globalization process, encouraging the formation of commercial blocs. There is reason to conclude, however, that the acceleration of the Latin American move toward integration is largely a result of the policy shift from protectionist policies and import substitution strategies to the opening up of these economies to external competition. As for the South American countries, analysis of recent events reveals two distinct features of these developments. First, trade liberalization is proceeding at two rates, one for imports from the region and another for imports from the rest of the world. Second, these are two mutually reinforcing processes.

Trade negotiations within MERCOSUR and GRAN have progressed rapidly during the 1990s and, thus far, the results have proved reasonably consistent with the objectives of eliminating all barriers to intra-group trade and converging toward a (low) common external tariff. In 1991, four of the GRAN countries (Peru withdrew from the negotiations) agreed that the process of tariff alignment with respect to third countries should be accomplished within a period of two years. More recently, in November 1994, a multi-tier tariff system, with a 20 per cent maximum, was negotiated, and the deadline for tariff convergence and intra-group tariff-free trade was set at February 1995. Some months earlier the presidents of the four MERCOSUR countries had agreed on establishing an (imperfect) customs union in January 1995.

Accompanying the move toward the integration of their markets, ambitious unilateral trade liberalization programs are being carried out by South American countries. Common program characteristics include drastic reduction of tariffs on extra-regional imports and simplification of tariff systems. At the start of the trade liberalization program (six or nine years ago, depending on the country), the maximum tariff for South American countries ranged from 65 per cent for Argentina to 220 per cent for Chile. By 1994, it ranged from 10 per cent for Bolivia to 40 per cent for Colombia and Ecuador (IDB, 1995). Concomitantly, the countries are reducing the number of tariff lines and dismantling the quantitative restrictions on imports. Some countries such as Chile and Bolivia have already made considerable headway in this regard. Chile has established a uniform tariff and eliminated all types of quantitative restrictions, while Bolivia has adopted a two-tier tariff-system and reduced import restrictions to a few bans and import licenses.

The current economic reform programs were formulated and first implemented in the 1980s. It led, in the 1990s, to a major transformation of the economic conditions of the MERCOSUR and GRAN countries and to the general reshaping of their integration framework. With overall trade liberalization, inter-country divergences in industrial protection levels notably narrowed substantially, facilitating within-group negotiations on a common tariff as well as tariff convergence between the two groups. By February 1995, the weighted-average CET was 11 per cent for MERCOSUR and 14 per cent for GRAN. Increased import exposure and the subsequent strengthening of foreign competition on the home market, in turn, made the advantages of having free access to neighbor markets more evident for local firms. This naturally made these firms less reluctant about the elimination of trade restrictions on intra-group trade. At present, about 90 per cent of intra-MERCOSUR trade and 80 per cent of intra-GRAN trade is tariff-free. However, certain obstacles to the full harmonization of South American countries' import policies will remain for some time. These obstacles entail differences between GRAN and MERCOSUR in terms of the time schedule for eliminating exclusion lists, the list of products which should be subject to common tariffs, the items included in one or another CET category and, not least, the regulations concerning domestic content and rules of origin.

Notwithstanding these advancements in economic integration and trade liberalization, the risk for the fragmentation of the region remains high. Apart from unresolved border conflicts, and differing opinions about the way to approach negotiations between GRAN and MERCOSUR (group-to-group or group-to-country), there is also the problem of sizeable divergences between and within groups in terms of macroeconomic performance and policy, particularly as concerns inflation and exchange rates. As we argue in subsequent sections, this problem constitutes, at present, one of the most serious obstacles to the consolidation of both GRAN and MERCOSUR and, consequently, to the fusion of these two into a larger trade bloc.

6.2 Increased Economic Interdependence

As the previous pattern of partial agreements and dispersed tariff negotiations within each country group and between pairs of countries is gradually replaced by the elimination of intra-group tariff and non-tariff barriers, and by the reduction of national tariffs on a global basis, the interdependence of South American economies increases. The rapid growth of intra-regional trade in the 1980s and the 1990s, as shown in Figure 6.1, is a clear indicator.

The extent to which this growth can be attributed to integration cannot be determined with any certainty; but the fact is that since the signing of the Asuncion Treaty and the relaunching of the GRAN agreement, intra-group trade has increased notably.

It more than doubled in the case of the MERCOSUR countries and increased by more than 60 per cent in the case of the GRAN countries.

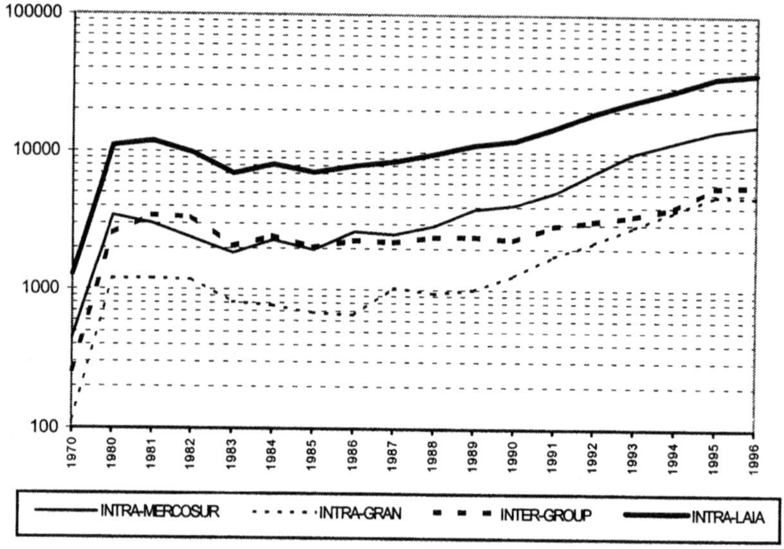

Figure 6.1. Intra-regional trade. MERCOSUR, GRAN and LAIA. Millions of current dollars. Computed on data from ECLAC (various years)

Growth in bilateral trade is also noteworthy. Trade between Colombia and Venezuela, for instance, already amounts to billions of dollars and continues to increase. Trade between Argentina and Brazil, in turn, has growth at a much faster rate than trade with other countries. In 1987, the year prior to the signing of the Argentine-Brazilian agreement, bilateral exports amounted to $1.2 billion. This represented less than 5 per cent of the total exports of the two countries. Six years later, bilateral exports had increased to $5.2 billion and their share in total exports to 13 per cent. Intra-group trade is important even for the smallest member countries. Paraguay's and Uruguay's trade with MERCOSUR partners, for example, accounted for more than 40 per cent of these countries' total trade in 1993.

The information provided in Table 6.1 reinforces the impression that integration has impacted positively on intra-regional trade. The figures in the table are average percentage shares of intra-group exports in total exports computed by reporting country over two periods: 1980-89 and 1990-96. Figures for the remaining LAIA members, that is, Mexico and Chile, are shown in the last rows of the table.

Table 6.1. Intra-regional trade. Percentage shares of intra-regional exports in total exports

	Within group		Within BLOC		Within LAIA	
	1980-89	1990-96	1980-89	1990-96	1980-89	1990-96
1 MERCOSUR	***7.6***	***17.0***	*11.8*	*21.5*	*14.8*	*31.1*
Argentina	10.7	26.6	15.6	31.8	19.1	44.1
Brazil	5.3	11.4	9.4	15.7	12.4	23.9
Paraguay	37.6	47.5	39.1	49.9	43.9	67.8
Uruguay	27.3	41.8	28.7	44.3	29.8	58.4
2 GRAN	***3.9***	***9.0***	*8.2*	*12.8*	*10.2*	*18.2*
Bolivia	3.9	15.6	47.7	37.9	50.5	55.5
Colombia	7.9	14.2	9.3	15.9	11.3	21.5
Ecuador	5.3	8.2	8.4	10.2	11.3	18.6
Peru	6.4	7.5	10.2	12.1	12.8	20.1
Venezuela	2.0	6.6	5.3	10.5	7.0	14.0
3 BLOC (1+2)	-	-	***10.3***	***18.3***	*12.9*	*26.3*
Chile	-	-	-	-	15.8	20.9
Mexico	-	-	-	-	3.9	4.0
LAIA					***10.8***	***18.2***

Source: ECLAC (various years)

For comparative purposes, export shares corresponding to LAIA and a hypothetical MERCOSUR-GRAN bloc have also been calculated. According to the table, the average share of intra-regional exports in total exports increased for all country groups and for all the individual. The largest increases were recorded within MERCOSUR, particularly as regard Argentina's and Uruguay's trade with partners. The weight of intra-bloc exports in total bloc exports has also increased but this has mostly depended on MERCOSUR countries' expanding regional exports. Note, however, that figures for the GRAN countries are not entirely comparable to those for the MERCOSUR countries as the former are oil exporters with extra-regional markets the main outlet for these exports.[1]

Direct investment flows among South American countries have also increased. As can be seen in Figure 6.2, the moderate growth of direct investment flows between and within MERCOSUR and GRAN during the 1980s transformed into accelerated growth in the early 1990s. The stock of investment indeed increased fourfold in the case of within-MERCOSUR investment and twofold in the cases within-GRAN and between-group investments. Even if this phenomenon can be seen as part of the general trend toward increased foreign capital flows into the

[1] The same is true in the case of Mexico.

region, the fact remains that intensification of regional interdependence in terms of investments is clearly taking place. This is particularly true in the case of MERCOSUR, where the proportion of within-group investments in total foreign-owned investment stocks grew from 0.4 per cent during the 1980s to 2 per cent during the 1990s.

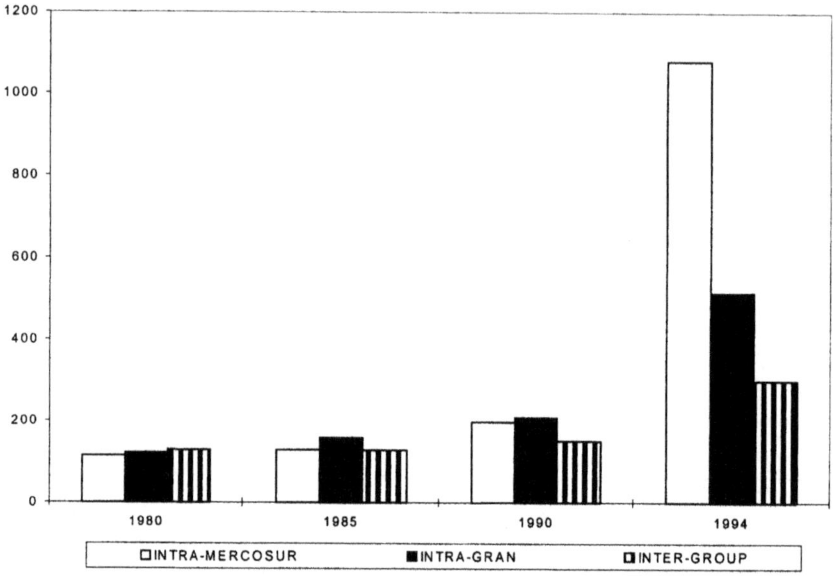

Figure 6.2. Intra and inter-group direct investment. GRAN and MERCOSUR. Stocks in millions of current dollars. Computed on data from IDB/IRELA (1996)

6.3 Disparities in Monetary Conditions and Stabilization Measures

Increased economic interdependence usually leads to increased sensitivity of the individual country's economy to changes in the other countries' economic conditions. Accordingly, discrepancies in the timing and extent of stabilization policies may become an obstacle to further advances in economic integration. In the case of the South American countries, one of the most obvious problems in this connection consists of large and endemic inter-country disparities in inflation and real exchange rates.

6.3.1 Inflation Rates

Figure 6.3 illustrates the first issue by providing the coefficients of variation of inflation rates for the GRAN and MERCOSUR member countries for the 1970-1997 period.

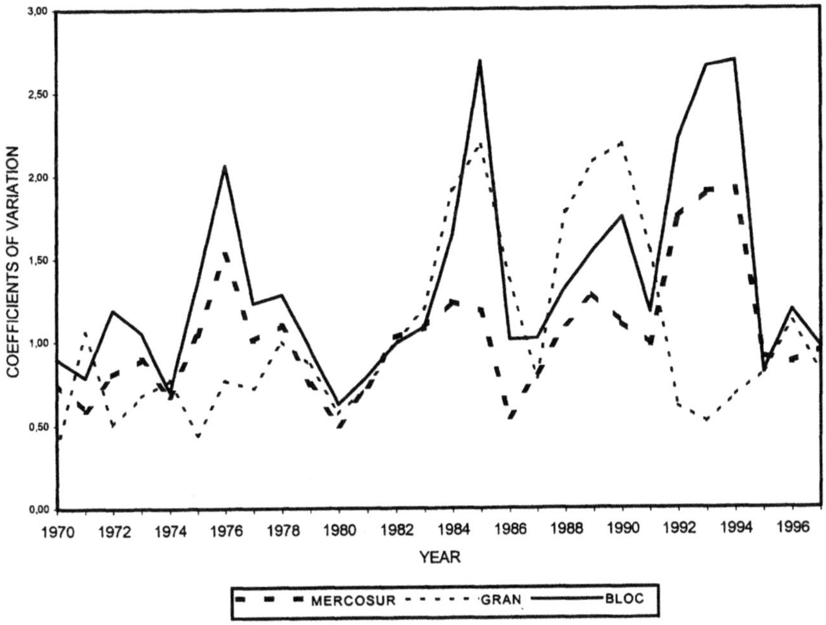

Figure 6.3. Disparities in inflation rates. GRAN, MERCOSUR and BLOC. 1970-1997. Coefficients of variation of annual average rates. Computed on data from ECLAC (various years)

As shown by the figure, there is a considerable increase in the degree of disparity, as measured by these coefficients in the 1980s, as compared with that prevailing in the previous decade. After reaching a peak in 1985, the degree of disparity tended to diminish, but it was increased again two years later, as inflation turned to hyperinflation in Argentina and Bolivia, and reached new records in Brazil and Peru. As a consequence, a new peak was reached in 1990 and 1993 for GRAN and MERCOSUR respectively. Note, however the recurring downward trend for the GRAN countries in 1992-1993 and for the MERCOSUR countries in 1994-1995. Note, finally, that even if the coefficient of variation for the GRAN-MERCOSUR bloc fluctuates somewhat after 1985, the trend is consistently upwards. In 1993, inflation rates ranged from 8.5 per cent (Bolivia) to 2100 per cent (Brazil). This represented a considerable increase in the degree of disparity as compared with the beginning of the 1980s.

6.3.2 Exchange Rates

The high degree of disparity in the rate of inflation among South American countries coupled with discrepancies in both balance of payments position and the timing of stabilization programs (see below) has produced major divergences in exchange rate movements.

Comparison of Figures 6.4 and 6.5 below shows that, on the whole, these divergences have been greater for the MERCOSUR countries than for the GRAN.

As shown in Figure 6.4, the exchange rates of the GRAN countries, not including Peru, tended to move closer together and depreciate during the 1985-1993 period, though certain differences can be noted, for instance between 1987 and 1988 and between 1991 and 1995.

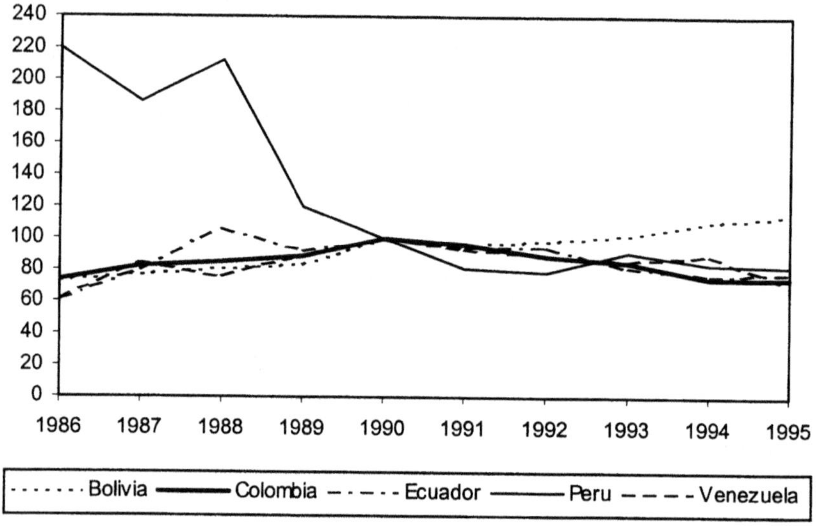

Figure 6.4. Real effective exchange rates. GRAN countries. Computed on data from ECLAC (various years)

The largest divergence from a regional common pattern was recorded in Peru. Between 1986 and 1989 this country's currency appreciated by 100 per cent in real terms. The trend continued until 1991, when Peru's real exchange rate reached its lowest level, slightly above one half of the 1989 rate. Thereafter, appreciation pressures weakened somewhat, mainly as a result of the stabilization program launched in 1992. This combined with the appreciation of the other countries' currency over the last two years to reduce the Peruvian misalignment with respect to its GRAN partners.

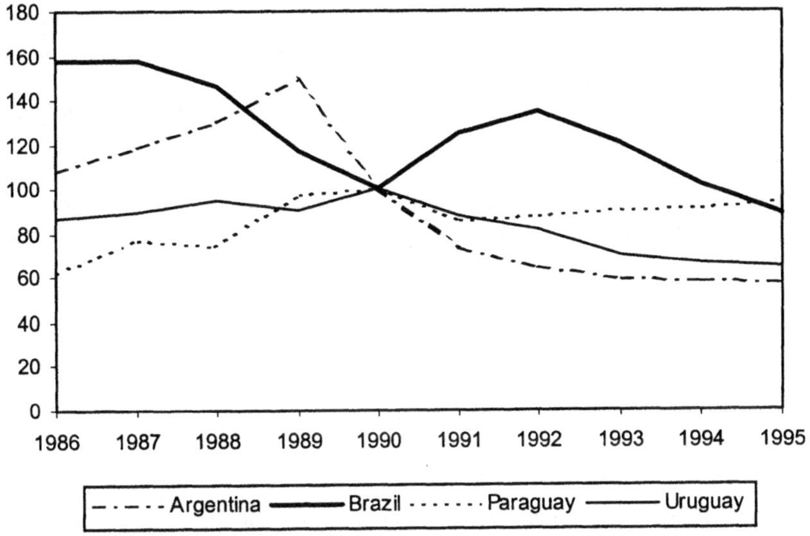

Figure 6.5. Real effective exchange rates. MERCOSUR countries. Computed on data from ECLAC (various years)

Figure 6.5 depicts a more complex situation for the MERCOSUR countries. As illustrated by the figure, the exchange rates of Argentina, Uruguay and Paraguay tended to depreciate during the late 1980s, but at very different pace in each case. Conversely, during the same period, the Brazilian currency is known to have appreciated.

After 1989, the Paraguayan and Uruguayan currencies tended to appreciate, although not as markedly as the Argentine one. The largest disparity in exchange rate movements was between the Argentine *peso* and the Brazilian *cruzado*. While the former appreciated by more than 50 per cent between 1989 and 1993, the latter depreciated by about 25 per cent. These abrupt changes in parities can be seen as transitory in that they were caused by differences in the timing of stabilization policies; but the fact is they are likely to pose additional obstacles to the integration of national markets.

6.3.3 Stabilization Policies

As shown in *Chapter 5*, moderate changes in regional parities greatly distort demand patterns and trade flows, eroding efforts for establishing fair rules of competition on the prospective common market. Moreover, they tend to reduce the welfare gains from tariff-free trade and, what is more important, the output impact of the simple abolition of tariffs. In recent years, these problems have been aggravated by the lack of coordination in the implementation of stabilization measures. This has led to renewed protectionist pressures which, on several occasions, have been strong enough to block negotiations or to produce additional limitations to the number of liberalized items, unilateral increases in custom duties and delays in the establishment of the planned customs union. Two illustrative episodes are Argentina's disguised increase in tariffs on MERCOSUR partners and Peru's withdraw from GRAN negotiations.

In 1990, the Argentine Government launched its Convertibility Plan, which anchored the *peso* to a fixed parity with the dollar. This plan has been successful in the sense that inflation has been controlled, the fiscal position improved and confidence in the national currency and the financial system restored. It was expected that Argentina's successful stabilization efforts would initially lead to appreciation of the *peso* and that this in turn would create an excess demand for traded goods, reduce the competitiveness of domestic producers and produce large trade deficits (Calvo and Végh, 1994). But it was also expected that increased productivity, decreasing prices for non-tradable goods and the improvement in the investment climate would, in the longer run, boost exports and alleviate pressure on the balance of payments. From a MERCOSUR perspective, however, the real problem emerged when the Brazilian economy failed to stabilize, at a time when both Brazil and Argentina were proceeding to dismantle all reciprocal trade barriers.

By 1989, the gap in Argentina/Brazil's relative prices was 48 percentage points favoring Argentina. One year later, the gap shrank to 5 percentage points. It reverted to 10 percentage points in favor of Brazil in 1991 and moved in that direction during 1992-1993 as the Argentine *peso* continued to appreciate *vis à vis* the Brazilian *cruzado*. Figure 6.4 shows that the consequence of this has been impressive growth in Brazilian exports to Argentina unmatched by an equivalent increase in Argentine exports to Brazil.

In 1992, Argentina's deficit in trade with Brazil neared $1.5 billion, and this induced the Argentine government to increase the so-called statistical tax on imports from 3 to 10 per cent in order to protect local firms from Brazilian competition and to alleviate balance of payments pressures. From an Argentine perspective there was good cause for increasing the statistical tax, but the fact is that it provoked a crisis within MERCOSUR. Uruguay protested against the Argentine decision, considering it a violation of the Asuncion Treaty, while Paraguay threatened to withdraw from MERCOSUR. The deficit shrank to $800 million in 1993 and $600 million in 1994, but the prospects for attaining balance in bilateral trade the following year were still uncertain. This motivated the decision of the Argentine Government to re-introduce in 1993 quotas on the import of certain manufactured products from MERCOSUR partners. Brazil promptly retaliated by canceling its preference margin on the imports of Argentine capital goods, but the risk of escalating protectionist measures was finally averted.

After the Brazilian Government decision, in July 1994, to introduce a new currency (the *real*) pegged to the dollar, Brazilian inflation fell dramatically. As a result, the Brazilian currency appreciated considerably *vis-à-vis* the Argentine.

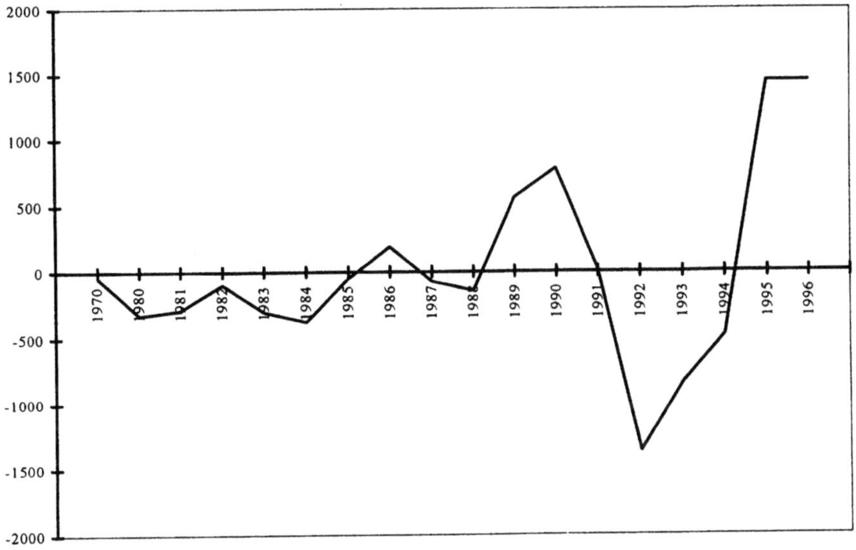

Figure 6.6. Balance of bilateral exports. Argentina-Brazil. Millions of current dollars. Computed on data from ECLAC (various years)

This. might have reduced the gap in relative prices, but the fact is that the financial situation in both countries has not significantly improved and the objective of policy harmonization continues to be a matter for discussion rather than a guide for concrete action. Hence, the risk of sudden and large movements in regional parities continues to be high

Another example of the damaging effects of uncoordinated economic reforms on integration efforts is Peru's virtual suspension of active participation in the group negotiations since 1992. The authors of a recent study (Reynolds et al, 1993) advance the hypothesis that growing interest rates resulting from Peru's current adjustment policy have combined with external factors, such as the improvement in capital markets, to produce a rapid increase in short-term capital inflows. This would have provoked Dutch Disease in the Peruvian economy, meaning that government efforts to prevent appreciation of the national currency, to improve export performance have been unsuccessful. As a consequence of the resulting steady decrease in Peru's competitiveness *vis-à-vis* the other GRAN countries, there has been a great reluctance on the part of the Peruvian Government to subordinate the implementation of its own economic reform program to the attainment of integration objectives. This is particularly true in the case of the elimination of all barriers to intra-regional trade and the establishment of a low common tariff.

6.4 Divergences in Economic Performance

The magnitude of the disparities in GDP per capita within GRAN and MERCOSUR has often been depicted as one of the most serious obstacles to further economic integration. It has been argued, for instance, that, in the absence of some form of institutionalized redistribution of income among participating countries, these disparities provide motive for perpetuating exceptions for the weaker members in "sensitive sectors" and make the countries unable to agree on a common trade policy. This type of problem was one of the causes of the failure of the LAFTA in the 1960s and the 1970s, when complicated regulations tended to substitute the market as the main mechanism for resource allocation at the regional level, ultimately leading to the breaking down of the free trade area project. This risk is still present in current integration efforts.

6.4.1 Income Disparities

Income disparities within both MERCOSUR and GRAN are approached in Table 6.2 by means of the percentage ratios of each member country's GDP per capita to the group average.

Table 6.2. MERCOSUR and GRAN Countries. GDP per capita as percentage of group average. 1990 constant dollars

	1986	1987	1988	1989	1990	1991	1992	1993	1994	1995
MERCOSUR										
Argentina	173	171	168	159	160	167	172	174	176	171
Uruguay	95	99	100	103	105	104	107	106	107	106
Brazil	88	87	87	90	86	82	77	76	75	79
Paraguay	44	44	46	48	49	47	45	44	42	44
GRAN										
Venezuela	170	170	177	171	178	184	189	184	173	171
Peru	131	138	123	113	105	103	98	101	111	113
Colombia	77	78	80	88	89	86	87	88	90	91
Ecuador	77	68	74	78	77	77	77	76	77	75
Bolivia	46	45	46	50	51	51	50	50	50	50
GRAN average as percentage of MERCOSUR average										
	55	54	55	52	54	54	52	51	50	52

Source: ECLAC (various years)

As concerns the MERCOSUR countries, the figures for Uruguay indicate a steady rise. Those for Brazil reflect a sharp downward trend since 1990, while Paraguay's position remains relatively stable at around 45 percent of the MERCOSUR average. Argentina's ratio, after steadily falling throughout the 1980s, recovered its initial level at the end of the period. The general impression is that the degree of disparity in GDP per capita among MERCOSUR countries has not changed dramatically between 1985 and 1993. As shown in the table, the overall range between the highest (Argentina) and the lowest income country (Paraguay) remained almost unchanged and no rank reversal was recorded during this period. Note, however, that the income gap between the two higher-income countries Argentina and Uruguay and the two lower-income ones Brazil and Paraguay tended to increase during the post-integration period. As for GRAN, there is clear evidence of increased income disparity. According to the table, a two-tier GRAN emerged in the late 1980s, and this trend became even more pronounced in the 1990s when Colombia ranked third in the group, but converged with Peru , and the gap between the upper and lower tiers (Ecuador and Bolivia) widened significantly. Note, finally, that the fusion of the two groups in an trade bloc would make it considerably more difficult to achieve income convergence. With the exception of Venezuela, and this depending on this country's large oil revenues, all GRAN countries have a level of GDP per capita well below the MERCOSUR average and slightly below that of Paraguay, the less developed of the MERCOSUR countries. As the last row in the table suggests, the income gap between the two groups remained almost stable during the period, reaching a maximum in 1990-1991.

6.4.2 Rates of Growth

Disparities in income per capita can be translated in terms of discrepancies in the growth rates of both output and population. On this approach, it seems evident, that when the latter tend to converge, divergences in the former have larger implications for income equalization. In fact, this is what has actually occurred within the GRAN-MERCOSUR bloc.

In Table 6.3, countries have been classified according to their average population growth rates. Comparison of the results, for the three periods considered in the table, reveals that, in general, population is growing slower and inter-countries differences in population growth rates are contracting. Under these circumstances, the emergence of a strongly inverse relationship between the ranking of the countries according to GDP per capita and the ranking by rate of output growth is required if income differences are to be progressively reduced. As the information provided by the table indicates, this has not been the case. The output growth pattern has been such that promoted income convergence in the 1970s and 1980s, but only to a limited extent. Countries in the lowest-income category, such as Peru and Bolivia often had a poor growth record, while countries in the middle category ranked high on the growth table. The pattern appears, however, fairly consistent with the objective of income equalization when it comes to the countries in the high-income category, particularly Argentina and Uruguay. Interestingly enough, the growth pattern accentuated its anti-income-equalization bias during the post-integration period, precisely when the convergence of population growth rates was becoming more evident. Of the low-income countries, only Bolivia came out at the highest end of the ranking, while

Table 6.3. MERCOSUR and GRAN countries. Classified according to income level and ranked according to average annual rates of growth

Country	1970-1980			1981-1990			1991-1993		
	GDP growth		Population	GDP growth		Population	GDP growth		Population
	Rate	Rank	growth[a]	Rate	Rank	growth[a]	Rate	Rank	growth[a]
High-income									
Argentina	2.5	8	A	-0.9	8	A	7.9	1	A
Venezuela	4.3	4	D	0.8	5	C	5.3	2	B
Uruguay	3.0	7	A	0.3	6	A	3.9	3	A
Middle-income									
Brazil	8.9	1	B	1.4	4	B	1.6	9	A
Paraguay	8.7	2	D	3.1	2	D	2.5	7	C
Colombia	5.5	3	B	3.5	1	B	3.5	5	A
Low-income									
Peru	3.6	6	C	-1.2	9	B	2.4	8	B
Ecuador	8.7	2	C	1.8	3	C	3.3	6	B
Bolivia	3.9	5	B	0.0	7	B	3.7	4	B

[a] Population growth rate intervals: A < 2, 2<B<2.5, 2.5<C<3, 3<D
Source: ECLAC (various years)

Argentina and Uruguay, which traditionally had a poor growth record among the fastest-growing countries during the period. It should be noted, however, that the output growth pattern actually promoted the convergence of income levels among the middle-income countries, namely Brazil, Paraguay and Colombia.

6.4.3 External Performance

While most South American countries have made considerable progress in trade liberalization and have benefited from the re-structuring of their foreign debts, there remain large cross-country differences in both the level of indebtedness and the degree of economic openness. Figure 6.7 compares these two indicators in two different periods, 1985-89 and 1990-93. The plots are based on the respective averages for these years.

As illustrated in the figure, the degree of openness increased for all the countries included in the sample between the two periods, with the largest increases recorded for Colombia, Bolivia, Uruguay and Ecuador. This accentuated the tendency toward the division of the countries into two clearly differentiated groups: one of increasingly open economies composed primarily of small countries and one of relatively closed economies made up of large and middle-size countries. Changes in the debt ratio are also pronounced when analyzed at the country level, but the resulting trend is now towards convergence with most of the ratios nearing the 30 per cent level.

The persistence of inter-country differences in the degree of economic openness[2] can be seen as a barrier to integration to the extent that it constitutes

[2] Defined as the percentage ratio of total trade to GDP at constant 1990 prices.

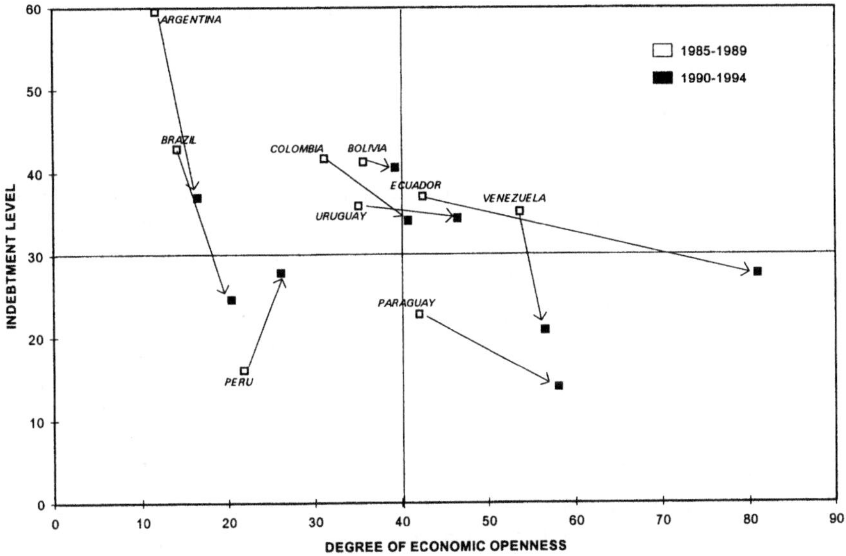

Figure 6.7. Level of indebtedness and degree of economic openness. Members of GRAN and MERCOSUR. Comparison of 1985-89 and 1990-94 averages. Computed on data from IDB (various years)

one of the main sources of discord among countries regarding the intensity and quality of the economic effects produced by policy shifts. Clearly, small countries such as Uruguay and Paraguay rank at the highest end of the scale. They are more dependent on trade with partners and, thus, more committed to bargaining on policy targets as a means of attaining integration objectives. Conversely, large countries such as Argentina and Brazil are more reluctant to engage in policy negotiations. The reason is simple. Since large countries normally have a low degree of economic openness, policy makers often see spillover and feedback effects from abroad as marginal. Accordingly, they are likely to neglect the effects of changes in partners' conditions on their own economies and instead base policy changes on domestic considerations.

Conversely, overall improvements in countries' level of indebtedness[3] make less difficult for countries to reach a point where common rules governing foreign investment and capital movements are seen as compatible with domestic conditions. Certainly, convergency to lower debt ratios would make countries equally attractive for foreign investment, particularly large-scale investment which attempts to benefit from the abolition of barriers to intra-regional trade, since all

[3] Defined as the percentage ratio of total debt service to exports at current prices

these economies are now able to maintain continuous access to world capital markets. This should, in part, counteract investment diversions within the region and therefore reduce the risk of a larger income gap among the countries and unfair distribution of integration benefits.

6.5 Concluding Remarks

Analysis of both intra-regional trade and the flows of mutual investment show that economic interdependence among South American countries is increasing. This raises some questions about the future of integration in the region. With growing economic interdependence, the likelihood of national economic cycles synchronizing and merging into a regional one also increases. Under such circumstances, the destabilizing effects of sudden external shocks and/or inconsistent shifts in domestic policy on one country are likely to be rapidly transmitted to the other countries, diminishing the prospects for regional growth and, therefore, undermining the conditions for further integration. Certainly, the stabilization efforts of one country may be efficient at the national level; but, as illustrated by the examples presented in this study, they may have a detrimental effect on the associate countries' balance of payments, thereby jeopardizing the common objective of achieving a fully integrated regional market.

The fact is, however, that South American countries are implementing similar economic reform programs and, in some cases, such as Argentina, Bolivia and Brazil, these have produced excellent results in terms of macroeconomic stability and even had a positive impact on neighbors' economic conditions. This could reinforce the notion that the lack of formal co-ordination mechanisms does not in itself constitute an insurmountable obstacle to the convergence of monetary conditions and that the individual country actually has the ability to steer effective anti-cyclical policies alone. Still, the persistence of major disparities in the evolution of real exchange rates reduces the likelihood of a regional "virtuous circle" emerging spontaneously in which stabilization measures adopted by diverse countries automatically reinforce each other and dilemmas between national and regional interest are avoided. It is therefore imperative to establish regional institutions and rules in the short term, which provide for political commitments regarding fiscal, monetary and balance of payments targets. To my understanding this is a prerequisite for both the consolidation of GRAN and MERCOSUR and the eventual fusion of the two into a South American Free Trade Area.

The persistence of large divergences in per capita income among South American countries tends to exacerbate the conflict over the allocation of the gains resulting from the integration of their economies. In principle, there is no reason to assume that market forces alone can ensure a fair distribution of these gains, meaning a distribution that benefits the relatively less-developed countries. On the other hand, designing mechanisms for regional distribution, fashioned after those implemented by EC countries, appears unrealistic given the limited extent of regional surpluses and the fact that regional institutions are still in the first stages of their development. For that very reason, the present study turned to analysis of the pattern of regional growth and posed the more general question of whether that pattern did or did not favor the reduction of income disparities, concluding that it did not. It was furthermore concluded that the merging of GRAN and MERCOSUR into a free trade area would only aggravate the problem.

The last issues analyzed were changes in indebtedness levels and in the degree of economic openness. It was understood that the amplification of inter-country divergences in both indicators would raise additional obstacles to the negotiation of common policy objectives and therefore to the full integration of South American markets. The results pointed to a considerable reduction in divergences in indebtedness levels. This trend would favor integration efforts to the extent that it facilitates a consensus regarding the sources of economic disequilibrium, and diminishes the risk of investment diversions. On the other hand, the increasing divergence in the degree of economic openness weakens the position of the smaller (and more open) countries in any negotiation on the parameters of economic policy, as it reinforces the propensity of the larger (and closer) economies to individually establish said parameters.

Methodological Appendix

Chapter 3

Rates of Growth

The rate of growth of total intra-MERCOSUR trade in the 1975-1990 period has been calculated as the difference between the unit and the antilogarithm of the coefficient b as estimated by the linear regression:

$$c_t = a + b_t + e_t \,, \tag{A1}$$

where c_t and a are the logarithms of the value of trade in year t and in the initial year, respectively.

Coefficients of Intra-Industry Trade

In the following formulas, i stands for the relevant industry, j for the reporting country, k for the trading partner, X for exports, and M for imports.

Grubel and Lloyd (GL)

By industry, country and trading partner:

$$GL_{ijk} = 100 \frac{\sum_k X_{ijk} + \sum_k M_{ijk} - \left| \sum_k X_{ijk} - \sum_k M_{ijk} \right|}{\sum_k X_{ijk} + \sum_k M_{ijk}} \,. \tag{A2}$$

By industry, country and groups of trading partners:

$$GB_{ij}^{k} = 100 \frac{\sum_k X_{ijk} + \sum_k M_{ijk} - \left| \sum_k X_{ijk} - \sum_k M_{ijk} \right|}{\sum_{ijk} \left[X_{ijk} + M_{ijk} \right]} \,. \tag{A3}$$

By groups of industries, countries and/or trading partners:

$$GL_{ij}^{k} = 100 \frac{\sum_{ijk} X_{ijk} + \sum_{ijk} M_{ijk} - \left| \sum_{k} X_{ijk} - \sum_{k} M_{ijk} \right|}{\sum_{ijk} \left[X_{ijk} + M_{ijk} \right]}. \tag{A4}$$

Aquino (Q)

The Aquino adjustment for bilateral flows of a specific industry is as follows:

$$Q_{ijk} = \frac{X'_{ijk} + M'_{ijk} - \left| X'_{ijk} + M'_{ijk} \right|}{X'_{ijk} + M'_{ijk}}, \tag{A5}$$

where

$$X'_{ijk} = X_{ijk} \frac{\sum_{i} X_{ijk} + \sum_{i} M_{ijk}}{\sum_{i} X_{ijk}}, \text{ and} \tag{A6}$$

$$M'_{ijk} = M'_{ijk} \frac{\sum_{i} X_{ijk} + \sum_{i} M_{ijk}}{\sum_{i} M_{ijk}}. \tag{A7}$$

As in the case of the GL index, the AQ indices can be aggregated for a group of industries, countries or trading partners. The formula for aggregation by industry is as follows:

$$Q_{jk}^{i} = 100 \frac{\sum_{i} X_{ijk} + \sum_{i} M_{ijk} - \left| \sum_{i} X'_{ijk} - \sum_{i} M_{ijk} \right|}{\sum_{i} X_{ijk} + \sum_{i} M_{ijk}}. \tag{A8}$$

Note that

$$\sum_{i} X'_{ijk} + \sum_{i} M'_{ijk} = \sum_{i} \left[X_{ijk} + M_{ijk} \right]. \tag{A9}$$

Chapter 5

Demand function (5.2) in the text is derived from the sub-utility function:

$$Y_j = \left[\sum_i a_{ij}^{1/\varepsilon} n_i m_i x_{ij}^{(\varepsilon - 1/\varepsilon)} \right]^{\varepsilon/(\varepsilon - 1)}, \varepsilon > 1, j = 1, \ldots, I. \quad \text{(A10)}$$

The function shows constant elasticity of substitution and it is separable between the homogeneous and differentiated products.

As mentioned in the text, the functional form of e_{ij} and q_{ij} depends on the choice of the output game. The following expressions are obtained from differentiating demand and inverse demand functions with respect to p_{ij} and m_i, respectively. Changes are incorporated through the price index q_j (3) for Bertrand behavior and alternatively through the sub-utility function Y_j for Cournot behavior.

Bertrand

$$e_{ij} = e-(e-m)s_{ij}, \text{ and} \quad \text{(A11)}$$

$$\theta_{ij} = \frac{\left[(1-\omega_i) s_{ij} + \omega_i\right](\varepsilon - \mu)}{e_{ij}(\varepsilon - 1)}. \quad \text{(A12)}$$

Cournot

$$e_{ij} = \frac{\varepsilon\mu}{\left[\mu(\mu - \varepsilon)s_{ij}\right]}, \text{ and} \quad \text{(A13)}$$

$$\theta_{ij} = \frac{\left[(1-\omega_i) s_{ij} + \omega_i\right](\varepsilon - \mu)}{\mu(\varepsilon - 1)}.$$

The cost function is assumed to be the same for all firms. It is given by

$$C(x_i, m_i) = c\,[\, z\,(c_0 + m_i c_m + m_i x_i) + (1-z)\,(m_i x_i^{a})^{b}], \quad \text{(A14)}$$

where z and $(1-z)$ are the weights and c, c_0, c_m, a, b are the cost parameters.

Statistical Appendix

Table A1. Matrix of intra-MERCOSUR exports of manufactures. Five-year averages in millions of current US dollars

Country of origin		Destination: Argentina	Brazil	Paraguay	Uruguay
1975-79	*Argentina*	0.00	132.92	64.59	82.03
	Brazil	197.88	0.00	169.77	77.74
	Paraguay	3.70	7.94	0.00	0.25
	Uruguay	37.32	36.32	4.07	0.00
1980-84	*Argentina*	0.00	148.51	64.25	84.35
	Brazil	403.31	0.00	280.94	247.46
	Paraguay	8.35	6.82	0.00	0.16
	Uruguay	78.35	36.75	6.88	0.00
1985-89	*Argentina*	0.00	2870.00	33.33	121.96
	Brazil	569.70	0.00	294.36	156.55
	Paraguay	2.37	9.14	0.00	0.50
	Uruguay	71.43	108.91	40.00	0.00

Source: Own estimations based on COMTRADE data

Table A2. Matrix of intra-MERCOSUR imports of manufactures. Five-year averages in millions of current US dollars

Destination		Country of origin: Argentina	Brazil	Paraguay	Uruguay
1975-79	*Argentina*	0.00	177.30	3.64	33.16
	Brazil	144.51	0.00	10.14	37.61
	Paraguay	30.24	54.19	0.00	3.36
	Uruguay	68.91	69.26	0.60	0.00
1980-84	*Argentina*	0.00	546.56	4.42	86.91
	Brazil	160.75	0.00	16.74	39.66
	Paraguay	37.57	129.86	0.00	5.74
	Uruguay	77.71	139.10	0.33	0.00
1985-89	*Argentina*	0.00	531.99	2.30	79.26
	Brazil	313.76	0.00	22.25	162.62
	Paraguay	22.42	136.86	0.00	4.12
	Uruguay	105.16	202.59	0.43	0.00

Source: Own estimations based on COMTRADE data

Table A3. Spearman correlation coefficients for GL and Q IIT indices

	Reporting country			
Trading partner	Argentina	Brazil	Paraguay	Uruguay
1975				
Argentina	1.0000			
Brazil	0.9557**	1.0000		
Paraguay	0.9998**	0.9699**	1.0000	
Uruguay	0.9925**	0.9859**	n.d	1.0000
MERCOSUR	0.9725**	0.8845**	0.9984**	0.9913**
LAIA	0.9915**	0.9722**	1.0000**	0.9904**
EC	0.8586**	0.7313**	0.9974**	0.9980**
US	0.9107**	0.7086**	1.0000**	0.9998**
Others	0.8188**	0.6525**	0.9991**	0.9883**
All	0.7003**	0.5870**	0.9910**	0.9690**
1980				
Argentina	1.0000			
Brazil	0.9248**	1.0000		
Paraguay	0.9671**	0.9993**	1.0000	
Uruguay	0.9975**	0.9031**	0.9956**	1.0000
MERCOSUR	0.8916**	0.8382**	0.9878**	0.9375**
LAIA	0.9894**	0.9882**	1.0000**	0.9988**
EC	0.9084**	0.8279**	0.9982**	0.9929**
US	0.8833**	0.8561**	0.9999**	0.9913**
Others	0.9015**	0.9768**	0.9968**	0.9402**
All	0.7533**	0.9462**	0.9888**	0.9078**
1985				
Argentina	1.0000			
Brazil	0.9686**	1.0000		
Paraguay	0.9844**	0.9965**	1.0000	
Uruguay	0.9872**	0.9605**	0.9796**	1.0000
MERCOSUR	0.8721**	0.9405**	0.9976**	0.9293**
LAIA	0.9569**	0.9804**	0.9976**	0.9995**
EC	0.9449**	1.0000**	0.9971**	0.9934**
US	0.9693**	0.9027**	0.9989**	0.9926**
Others	0.9968**	0.8361**	0.9990**	1.0000**
All	0.9284**	0.8316**	0.9920**	0.9871**
1990				
Argentina	1.0000			
Brazil	0.9872**	1.0000		
Paraguay	0.9798**	0.9757**	1.0000	
Uruguay	0.9030**	0.9979**	0.9938**	1.0000
MERCOSUR	0.9332**	0.9998**	0.9658**	0.9479**
LAIA	0.8979**	0.9629**	0.9905**	0.9986**
EC	0.9839**	0.9832**	0.9949**	0.9924**
US	0.9941**	0.9563**	0.9938**	0.9999**
Others	0.9745**	0.8313**	0.9758**	0.9890**
All	0.9768**	0.8570**	0.9639**	0.9624**

Source: Own estimations based on COMTRADE data

Table A4. Intra-MERCOSUR exports according to SITC divisions. Percentage shares of member countries in total exports. Selected years

SITC	Argentina			Brazil			Paraguay			Uruguay		
	1980	1985	1990	1980	1985	1990	1980	1985	1990	1980	1985	1990
51	5.49	56.80	31.26	50.88	29.92	42.64	3.08	3.38	10.56	10.55	9.91	15.54
52	4.92	66.15	80.76	0.00	0.00	0.00	35.50	0.00	8.94	59.59	33.85	10.30
53	18.84	27.07	12.95	33.39	41.84	63.34	31.38	17.68	8.07	16.39	13.42	15.64
54	16.51	50.09	20.44	14.68	0.86	9.17	48.91	21.16	28.05	19.91	27.89	42.34
55	27.60	28.82	13.09	16.85	14.11	54.32	49.08	46.93	20.62	6.46	10.15	11.97
56	35.10	10.36	3.86	30.96	3.19	28.65	28.91	62.25	45.71	5.03	24.20	21.78
57	27.20	2.59	4.06	0.00	0.00	3.28	64.96	79.77	74.80	7.84	17.64	17.87
58	60.98	46.02	10.08	6.30	160.00	39.80	7.37	8.09	9.17	25.36	29.90	40.95
59	58.81	69.26	21.31	18.07	6.72	40.15	9.05	7.76	24.59	14.06	16.26	13.96
61	2.77	0.12	0 .43	45.60	91.03	66.43	4.80	0.08	0.16	46.84	8.76	32.98
62	38.01	28.71	5.21	23.82	9.54	40.97	32.79	56.44	47.17	5.38	5.32	6.65
63	54.64	33.54	6.07	29.37	32.64	77.71	3.08	18.38	2.82	12.90	15.44	13.40
64	73.61	51.09	21.40	0.20	4.70	49.79	18.19	20.30	12.23	80.00	23.92	16.58
65	44.07	24.22	8.21	8.16	9.35	51.10	38.78	52.85	26.83	90.00	13.58	13.86
66	49.65	17.13	11.16	10.90	2.82	41.79	35.20	68.80	360.00	4.24	11.25	11.05
67	51.71	61.94	33.78	7.74	0 .95	11.17	16.27	17.93	17.95	24.28	19.18	37.10

Table A4 (cont.). Intra-MERCOSUR exports according to SITC divisions. Percentage shares of member countries in total exports. Selected years

SITC	Argentina			Brazil			Paraguay			Uruguay		
	1980	1985	1990	1980	1985	1990	1980	1985	1990	1980	1985	1990
68	47.19	67.86	20.31	0.01	8.35	17.77	6.77	6.54	4.65	46.03	17.26	57.27
69	41.25	22.56	9.81	4.14	4.20	21.52	35.37	50.25	51.53	19.24	22.98	17.14
71	51.11	42.89	17.46	11.08	7.12	44.96	19.82	36.27	13.18	17.99	13.72	24.41
72	49.28	44.16	18.34	10.87	9.94	13.68	22.93	22.79	38.20	16.93	23.12	29.78
73	31.43	32.27	13.52	7.13	29.28	38.13	21.58	140.00	13.96	39.86	24.45	34.39
81	67.39	7.61	4.46	0.05	0.68	21.12	30.18	82.19	58.31	2.39	9.53	16.11
82	20.57	4.60	8.04	1.87	0.00	45.87	70.59	89.16	13.11	6.97	6.24	32.97
83	14.51	45.93	9.70	0.00	0.00	74.42	82.95	51.85	13.56	2.54	2.22	2.32
84	32.66	22.76	8.05	0.79	3.76	70.55	64.13	68.19	17.24	2.41	5.29	4.16
85	33.61	3.87	1.36	4.52	3.46	19.06	53.16	86.74	59.51	8.71	5.93	20.07
86	41.71	46.69	13.84	29.99	36.17	53.43	17.42	9.23	12.14	10.88	7.92	20.59
89	48.27	35.36	16.78	4.72	2.81	30.95	30.70	42.43	28.87	16.31	19.39	23.39

Source: Own estimations based on COMTRADE data

Table A5. Aquino-adjusted indices of MERCOSUR intra-industry trade by trading partner. SITC 5-8, calculated at the 3-digit level of aggregation

Trade flow		Reporting country				
		Argentina	Brazil[a]	Paraguay	Uruguay	MERCOSUR[a]
Intra-MERCOSUR						
Argentina	1975					
	1980					
	1985					
	1990					
Brazil	1975	37.12				
	1980	44.40				
	1985	39.60				
	1990	60.24				
Paraguay	1975	2.93	21.44.			
	1980	17.71	1.24.			
	1985	15.91	0.45.			
	1990	12.67	5.46.			
Uruguay	1975	33.96	13.08	0.00		
	1980	37.41	23.95	0.60		
	1985	42.93	380.00	0.00		
	1990	40.85	26.59	9.90		
MERCOSUR	1975	44.19	42.15	0.69	29.02	
	1980	56.19	45.63	2.21	39.61	
	1985	52.10	42.56	1.36	52.32	
	1990	63.27	53.97	7.47	47.14	
Extra-MERCOSUR						
LAIA	1975	17.30	22.36	1.43	10.21	23.72
	1980	33.81	19.80	0.93	8.04	26.99
	1985	37.78	27.70	0.80	10.81	360.00
	1990	40.53	22.32	5.31	19.30	30.81
EC	1975	32.12	27.27	0.89	4.64	31.48
	1980	29.29	31.62	0.98	5.14	38.37
	1985	27.86	47.46	1.72	11.33	50.29
	1990	40.78	39.95	1.77	11.49	41.68
US	1975	38.90	27.46	0.01	5.34	30.23
	1980	29.57	34.78	1.04	6.74	44.21
	1985	26.79	35.48	0.76	6.92	36.83
	1990	29.86	41.91	2.65	6.37	41.24
Others	1975	16.95	27.79	0.46	15.30	30.73
	1980	24.73	37.37	1.52	12.76	44.25
	1985	27.08	30.03	0.49	12.92	33.16
	1990	28.77	32.46	2.27	17.98	33.68
All	1975	390.00	42.49	20.00	21.09	46.62
	1980	50.98	46.18	2.79	30.05	59.18
	1985	48.63	47.75	1.48	32.78	52.86
	1990	51.29	48.83	6.06	34.46	52.99

[a] The 1990 indices correspond to 1989 data.

Source: Own estimations based on COMTRADE data

Table A6. Spearman correlation coefficients for GL- IIT indices. MERCOSUR as a whole. Computed at the 4-digit level of aggregation. 1989

Mercosur trade with	Argentina	Brazil	Paraguay	Uruguay	LAIA	EC	US	Others
Argentina	1.00							
Brazil	0.22**	1.00						
Paraguay	0.16*	0.06	1.00					
Uruguay	0.22**	0.38**	0.06	1.00				
LAIA	0.13	0.07	0.13	0.32**	1.00			
EEC	0.18**	0.06	0.03	0.17*	0.11	1.00		
US	0.15*	0.25**	-0.00	0.11	0.03	0.37**	1.00	
Others	0.20**	0.24**	0.02	0.23**	0.10	0.22**	0.38**	1.00
1975 vs *1989*	0.26**	0.27**	0.22**	0.19*	0.34**	0.18*	0.13	0.26*

Source: Own estimations based on COMTRADE data

Table A7. Spearman correlation coefficients for GL-IIT indices. By member country. Computed at the 4-digit level of aggregation. 1989

	All	MERCOSUR	LAIA	EC	US	Others
Argentina						
All	1.00					
MERCOSUR		0.32**	1.00			
LAIA	0.21**	0.32**	1.00			
EC	0.32**	0.28**	0.14*	1.00		
US	0.41**	0.30**	0.21**	0.41**	1.00	
Others	0.56**	0.21**	0.15*	0.28**	0.33**	1.00
Brazil						
All	1.00					
MERCOSUR	0.29**	1.00				
LAIA	0.20**	0.27**	1.00			
EC	0.51**	0.22**	0.14*	1.00		
US	0.46**	0.26**	0.19**	0.43**	1.00	
Others	0.61**	0.33**	0.24**	0.39**	0.39**	1.00
Paraguay						
All	1.00					
MERCOSUR	0.80**	1.00				
LAIA	0.56**	0.27*	1.00			
EC	0.58**	0.62**	0.15	1.00		
US	0.45**	0.55**	0.25*	0.73**	1.00	
Others	0.60**	0.73**	0.40**	0.75**	0.73**	1.00
Uruguay						
All	1.00					
MERCOSUR	0.80**	1.00				
LAIA	0.40**	0.37**	1.00			
EC	0.20*	0.19*	0.25**	1.00		
US	0.19*	0.15	0.23*	0.36**	1.00	
Others	0.57**	0.39**	0.39**	0.38**	0.32**	1.00

Source: Own estimations based on COMTRADE data

Table A8. Spearman correlation coefficients for Aquino-adjusted IIT indices. MERCOSUR as a whole. Computed at the 3-digit level of aggregation. 1989

	Argentina	Brazil	Paraguay	Uruguay	LAIA	EC	US	Others
Argentina	1.00							
Brazil	0.50**	1.00						
Paraguay	0.26*	0.32*	1.00					
Uruguay	0.39**	0.56**	0.19	1.00				
LAIA	0.26*	0.37**	0.26*	0.35**	1.00			
EC	0.33**	0.45**	0.11	0.28*	0.18	1.00		
US	0.17	0.33**	0.08	0.17	0.10	0.45**	1.00	
Others	0.18	0.40**	0.10	0.24*	0.32**	0.62**	0.74**	1.00
1975 vs 1989	0.40**	0.44**	0.20	0.44**	0.33**	0.12	0.06	0.31**

Source: Own estimations based on COMTRADE data

Table A9. Spearman correlation coefficients for Aquino-adjusted IIT indices. By member country. Computed at the 4-digit level of aggregation.

	All	MERCOSUR	LAIA	EC	US	Others
Argentina						
All	1.00					
MERCOSUR	0.32**	1.00				
LAIA	0.35**	0.29*	1.00			
EC	0.45**	0.24*	0.36**	1.00		
US	0.58**	0.28*	0.36**	0.44**	1.00	
Others	0.62**	0.11	0.21	0.28*	0.46**	1.00
Brazil						
All	1.00					
MERCOSUR	0.27*	1.00				
LAIA	0.18	0.37**	1.00			
EC	0.66**	0.23	0.11	1.00		
US	0.62**	0.16	0.07	0.51**	1.00	
Others	0.62**	0.36**	0.18	0.40**	0.47**	1.00
Paraguay						
All	1.00					
MERCOSUR	0.79**	1.00				
LAIA	0.51**	0.34*	1.00			
EC	0.58**	0.27	0.24	1.00		
US	0.42**	0.41**	0.37*	0.49**	1.00	
Others	0.62**	0.59**	0.51**	0.60**	0.67**	1.00
Uruguay						
All	1.00					
MERCOSUR	0.74**	1.00				
LAIA	0.40**	0.35**	1.00			
EC	0.15	0.14	0.21	1.00		
US	0.27*	0.17	0.20	0.49**	1.00	
Others	0.46**	0.27*	0.30*	0.48**	0.52**	1.00

Source: Own estimations based on COMTRADE data

Table A10. Classification of products according to factor intensity

5121	Hydrocarbons	HC/T
5125	Organic acids	HC/T
5142	Metal compounds of inorganic acid	HC/T
5310	Synthetic dyes	HC/T
5333	Prepared paints	HC/T
5542	Washing preparations	HC/T
5811	Products of condensation	HC/T
5812	Products of polymerizing	HC/T
5813	Cellulose derivatives	HC/T
5995	Starch, insulin, gluten	HC/T
5999	Chemical products	HC/T
6114	Leather bovine	NR
6291	Rubber tyres	HC/T
6535	Woven synthetic fabrics	UL
6554	Other coated textiles	UL
6770	Iron, steel wire	HC/T
6952	Tools	HC/T
7115	Piston engines non-air	HC/T
7143	Statistical machines	HC/T
7192	Pumps, centrifuges	HC/T
7193	Mechanical handling equipment	HC/T
7196	Nonelectrical machinery	HC/T
7199	Machine parts	HC/T
7221	Electric power machinery	HC/T
7222	Switchgear	HC/T
7231	Insulated wire, cable	HC/T
7250	Domestic electric equipment	HC/T
7299	Other electrical machinery	HC/T
7328	Motor vehicle parts	HC/T
8619	Measuring, controlling instruments	HC/T
8624	Photo film	HC/T
8921	Printed books	HC/T
8930	Articles of plastic	HC/T

Table A11. GL IIT indices for Argentina, Brazil and Uruguay. According to trading partners 1985. Selected ISIC industries)

				ISIC			
Trade flow	3513	3522	3691	3825	3831	3833	3843
Argentina							
Brazil	27.92	3.37	2.65	5.74	96.95	67.11	99.39
Uruguay	46.43	7.17	30.18	11.06	26.42	12.80	76.50
MERCOSUR	37.79	54.88	9.75	10.37	79.97	83.58	98.56
LAIA	54.88	14.56	22.09	97.42	14.57	29.61	59.69
Others	39.38	22.51	8.45	92.45	22.83	39.54	27.94
All	71.64	36.04	10.64	87.92	37.66	73.71	61.35
Brazil							
Argentina	27.92	3.37	2.65	5.74	96.95	67.11	99.39
Uruguay	99.22	12.67	83.10	2.08	72.64	4.06	0.23
LAIA	1.75	61.31	.17	6.55	5.63	0.27	14.57
MERCOSUR	63.85	4.98	33.45	5.54	82.35	95.72	79.35
Others	90.14	61.82	43.86	98.55	42.69	27.18	25.96
All	79.78	73.43	34.58	90.87	55.41	310.00	27.28
Uruguay							
Argentina	46.43	7.17	30.18	11.06	26.42	12.80	76.50
Brazil	99.22	12.67	83.10	2.08	72.64	4.06	.23
MERCOSUR	70.72	9.14	85.77	4.88	62.33	66.04	20.68
LAIA	7.05	31.17	13.43	7.18	23.58		
Others	5.16	27.03	0.80	2.05	26.65	1.35	37.86
All	87.13	31.67	34.48	2.73	54.51	79.58	24.54
MERCOSUR							
LAIA	30.24	44.35	0.78	43.87	6.74	4.42	21.08
Others	95.22	44.98	83.70	95.27	39.06	53.77	46.09
All	93.34	56.65	72.96	99.89	52.24	580.00	47.87

Source: Chapter 5.

Table A12. Correlations between additive model variables. Argentina. 1983

	PSD	MS	COSTS	EI	II
PSD	1.000	0.846^{**}	0.732^{**}	0.244	0.176
MS		1.000	0.863^{**}	0.254	-0.057
COSTS			1.000	0.145	0.143
EI				1.000	-0.373
II					1.000

1-tailed signif: * - .01, ** - 0.001. N of cases: 15

Table A13. Correlations between multiplicative model variables. Argentina 1984

	PSD	MS	CONC	PROD	EI	II
PSD	1.000	0.251	0.043	-0.082	-0.021	0.062
MS		1.000	-0.889**	-0.470**	-0.305*	0.243
CONC			1.000	0.396**	0.209	-0.343*
PROD				1.000	0.130	-0.080
EI					1.000	-0.365**
II						1.000

1-tailed signif: * - .01, ** - 0.001. N of cases: 79

Table A14. Correlations between multiplicative model variables. Brazil. 1985

	PSD	MS	CONC	PROD	EI	II
PSD	1.000	0.000	0.527**	0.430**	0.048	-0.226
MS		1.000	-0.764**	-0.139	-0.080	-0.204
CONC			1.000	0.304*	0.034	-0.281*
PROD				1.000	0.140	-0.012
EI					1.000	-0.215
II					1.000	

1-tailed signif: * - .01, ** - 0.001. N of cases: 79

Table A15. Correlations between multiplicative model variables. Uruguay. 1988

	PSD	*MS*	*CONC*	*PROD*	*EI*	*II*
PSD	1.000	0.263	0.139	0.114	0.058	-0.341*
MS		1.000	-0.789**	-0.571**	-0.046	-0.252
CONC			1.000	0.520**	-0.055	-0.238
PROD				1.000	0.196	0.127
EI					1.000	-0.135
II						1.000

1-tailed signif: * - .01, ** - 0.001. N of cases: 63

Table A16. Correlations between multiplicative model variables. Uruguay. 1978

	PSD	MS	CONC	PROD	EI	II
PSD	1.000	0.162	0.030	0.291	0.054	-0.192
MS		1.000	-0.898**	-0.266	-0.413*	-0.337*
CONC			1.000	0.417*	0.254	0.015
PROD				1.000	-0.193	-0.063
EI					1.000	0.079
II						1.000

1-tailed signif: * - .01, ** - 0.001. N of cases: 49

Table A17. Products in the sample and variable values. Variables estimated in physical terms. Argentina 1983

CIIU	Product	TRE	TRM	IE	II	CU
3133	Beer	0.105233	1.578500	1.000000	1.000000	0.140000
3140	Cigarettes	0.112067	0.784472	1.000000	1.000000	0.020000
3511	Petrochemicals	0.111660	3.068400	1.229506	0.841155	0.190000
3513	Synthetic fibers	0.027295	1.854524	1.023310	0.603746	0.140000
3523	Soaps	0.001261	0.585000	1.051867	0.557998	0.030000
3551	Tyres	0.035128	1.202215	1.053327	0.968140	0.070000
3692	Cement	0.267364	5.808520	1.012747	0.999742	0.380000
3710	Steel	0.137315	0.862222	1.168577	0.794459	0.110000
3822	Harvest mach.	0.009523	0.107900	1.021480	0.949954	0.100000
3822	Tractors	0.015048	0.092089	1.000615	0.979850	0.084000
3829	Refrigerators	0.050400	0.502628	1.002722	1.000000	0.110000
3829	Washing mach.	0,029000	0.290000	1.000000	1.000000	0.100000
3832	Television sets	0.036813	0.257692	1.000000	1.000000	0.050000
3843	Automobiles	0.024000	0.254676	1.039106	0.996073	0.150000
3843	Trucks	0.011409	0.125650	1.007570	0.991246	0.120000

Table A18. Products in the sample and variable values. Variables estimated in physical terms. Brazil. 1987

CIIU	Product	TRE	TRM	IE	II	CU
3133	Beer	0.310085	14.525815	1.003330	0.999976	0.140000
3140	Cigarettes	0.210298	4.193138	1.003051	1.000000	0.020000
3511	Ethylene	0.501008	1.535818	1.000000	0.978647	0.075000
3511	Sulfuric acid	0.191126	7.156434	1.000072	0.961380	0.075000
3513	Synthetic rubber	1.042911	3.505850	1.077076	0.823647	0.200000
3513	Synthetic fibers	0.025166	2.491750	1.083152	0.972299	0.100000
3513	Nylon	0.076676	1.186750	1.001315	0.967874	0.070000
3513	Acrylic fibers	0.252723	1.567227	1.008005	0.799821	0.140000
3513	Cellulosic fibers	0.173425	1.026770	1.035557	0.814490	0.070000
3513	Polyester	0.591288	3.300816	1.086298	0.982050	0.140000
3521	Paints	0.094108	9.510921	1.000274	0.999095	0.044000
3523	Detergents	0.017397	3.842586	1.024707	0.997929	0.030000
3551	Tyres	0.534894	4.505234	1.066152	0.997860	0.070000
3692	Cement	0.473167	22.754000	1.009731	0.988442	0.380000
3822	Harvest mach.	0.014903	0.454750	1.047599	0.998791	0.100000
3822	Tractors	0.096092	0.569911	1.153193	0.999454	0.084000
3829	Refrigerators	0.230856	4.376480	1.052144	0.999973	0.110000
3829	Washing mach	0.043108	0.857230	1.005809	0.999900	0.100000
3832	Television sets	0.092649	0.897867	1.198226	0.992798	0.050000
3843	Automobiles	0.086032	1.101768	1.085274	0.999975	0.150000
3843	Trucks	0.089146	0.384020	1.138537	0.999896	0.120000
3844	Bicycles	1.952097	21.502790	1.082308	0.999735	0.056000

Table A19. Simulation of trade liberalization. Basic data and parameters

ISIC 3513-Artificial and synthetic fibers. Market elasticity: 0.5; No. of sub-industries: 1

	Argentina	Brazil	Uruguay	ROL	ROW
No. of firms	11.00	17.00	4.00	32.00	159.00
Average firm[a]	25.45	110.82	8.00	68.63	68.61
Production[a]	280.00	1884.00	32.00	2196.00	10908.51
Consumption[a]	299.50	1843.04	34.24	2398.22	10725.51
Herfindahl index	0.066	0.054	0.128	0.025	0.006
ROW tariffs[b]	32.00	47.00	33.00	37.00	
Tariff reduction[b]					
Argentina	0.00	30.00	75.00	10.00	0.00
Brazil	30.00	0.00	75.00	10.00	0.00
Uruguay	87.00	75.00	0.00	10.00	0.00
ROL	10.00	10.00	10.00	0.00	0.00
ROW	0.00	0.00	0.00	0.00	0.00
Shares in production[b]					
Argentina	91.20	0.27	0.51	5.48	2.53
Brazil	0.25	93.54	0.14	1.08	4.99
Uruguay	14.85	8.31	76.35	0.04	0.44
ROL	0.26	0.01	0.02	97.58	2.13
ROW	0.27	0.71	0.05	2.01	96.96

Returns to scale

MOS[a] 68.63; increase in average costs at 1/2 output per model 10%, at 1/2 number of models 3%; linear/loglinear weights 0.5, 0.5

ISIC 3522-Pharmaceutical products. Market elasticity: 0.5; No. of sub-industries: 1

	Argentina	Brazil	Uruguay	ROL	ROW
No. of firms	48.00	68.00	25.00	141.00	1635.00
Average firm[a]	26.12	45.18	4.66	31.51	31.52
Production[a]	1253.93	3072.37	116.59	4442.89	51531.03
Consumption[a]	1326.48	3117.56	130.78	4799.99	51042.01
Herfindahl index	0.090	0.069	0.150	0.030	0.003
ROW tariffs[b]	9.00	27.00	21.00	19.00	
Tariff reduction[b]					
Argentina	0.00	30.00	50.00	10.00	0.00
Brazil	30.00	0.00	50.00	10.00	0.00
Uruguay	20.00	30.00	0.00	10.00	0.00
ROL	10.00	10.00	10.00	0.00	0.00
ROW	0.00	0.00	0.00	0.00	0.00
Shares in production[b]					
Argentina	98.37	0.01	0.15	0.59	0.88
Brazil	0.16	97.97	0.03	0.34	1.50
Uruguay	0.06	0.06	97.18	0.77	1.94
ROL	0.01	0.10	0.00	98.61	1.27
ROW	0.17	0.20	0.03	0.78	98.83

MOS[a] 31.51; increase in average costs at 1/2 output per model 22 %, at 1/2 number of models 5 %; linear/loglinear weights 1, 0

[a] million USD, [b] percentages , [c] from MERCOSUR average

Table A19 (cont.). Simulation of trade liberalization. Basic data and parameters

ISIC 3691-Bricks and other clay products. Market elasticity: 0.5; No. of sub-industries: 1

	Argentina	Brazil	Uruguay	ROL	ROW
No. of firms	48.00	28.00	10.00	86.00	164.00
Average firm[a]	3.72	55.64	0.54	20.25	20.27
Production[a]	178.65	1557.88	5.38	1741.91	3325.08
Consumption[a]	195.55	1522.92	2.82	1751.62	3335.98
Herfindahl index	0.017	0.035	0.059	0.011	0.006
ROW tariffs[b]	30.00	55.00	40.00	42.00	
Tariff reduction[b]					
Argentina	0.00	40.00	10.00	10.00	0.00
Brazil	40.00	0.00	10.00	10.00	0.00
Uruguay	95.00	50.00	0.00	10.00	0.00
ROL	10.00	10.00	10.00	0.00	0.00
ROW	0.00	0.00	0.00	0.00	0.00
Shares in production[b]					
Argentina	99.44	0.01	0.05	0.11	0.39
Brazil	0.10	97.16	0.04	0.69	2.01
Uruguay	8.68	7.58	39.80	2.32	41.62
ROL	0.00	0.00	0.00	97.52	2.47
ROW	0.48	0.26	0.00	1.26	98.00

MOS[a] 20.25; increase in average costs at 1/2 output per model 15 %, at 1/2 number of models 0 %; linear/loglinear weights 0.5 , 0.5

ISIC 3825-Office machinery. Market elasticity: 0.5; No. of sub-industries: 1

	Argentina	Brazil	Uruguay	ROL	ROW
No. of firms	5.00	43.00	11.00	59.00	295.00
Average firm[a]	32.89	57.72	0.23	44.90	44.95
Production[a]	164.43	2481.97	2.58	2648.98	13261.21
Consumption[a]	196.53	2442.54	10.72	3321.71	12587.68
Herfindahl index	0.027	0.039	0.013	0.018	0.006
ROW tariffs[b]	13.00	40.00	25.00	26.00	
Tariff reduction[b]					
Argentina	0.00	40.00	50.00	10.00	0.00
Brazil	40.00	0.00	50.00	10.00	0.00
Uruguay	25.00	20.00	0.00	10.00	0.00
ROL	10.00	10.00	10.00	0.00	0.00
ROW	0.00	0.00	0.00	0.00	0.00
Shares in production[b]					
Argentina	28.97	0.29	0.25	6.29	64.20
Brazil	0.66	90.50	0.04	1.18	7.62
Uruguay	0.93	0.27	95.70	0.46	2.63
ROL	0.37	0.04	0.01	90.42	9.16
ROW	0.93	1.47	0.05	6.69	90.87

MOS[a] 44.90; increase in average costs at 1/2 output per model 10 %, at 1/2 number of models 5 %; linear/loglinear weights 0.8 , 0.2

[a] million USD, [b] percentages , [c] from MERCOSUR average

Table A19 (cont.). Simulation of trade liberalization. Basic data and parameters

ISIC 3831-part- Electrical power machinery. Market elasticity: 0.5; No. of sub-industries: 1

	Argentina	Brazil	Uruguay	ROL	ROW
No. of firms	35.00	73.00	24.00	132.00	758.00
Average firm[a]	5.71	43.18	0.37	25.46	25.47
Production[a]	200.00	3151.83	8.92	3360.75	19304.58
Consumption[a]	252.86	3321.71	14.87	4289.51	18147.14
Herfindahl index	0.030	0.023	0.015	0.006	0.003
ROW tariffs[b]	22.00	38.00	28.00	29.00	
Tariff reduction[b]					
Argentina	0.00	30.00	30.00	10.00	0.00
Brazil	30.00	0.00	40.00	10.00	0.00
Uruguay	90.00	90.00	0.00	10.00	0.00
ROL	10.00	10.00	10.00	0.00	0.00
ROW	0.00	0.00	0.00	0.00	0.00
Shares in production[b]					
Argentina	92.02	1.22	0.94	1.59	4.23
Brazil	0.08	96.65	0.15	0.79	2.32
Uruguay	3.22	30.85	59.97	1.13	4.83
ROL	0.01	0.02	0.00	80.68	19.29
ROW	0.34	1.40	0.01	8.03	90.22

MOS[a] 25.46; increase in average costs at 1/2 output per model 15 %, at 1/2 number of models 5 %; linear/loglinear weights 0.8 , 0.2

ISIC 3833-29-part- Elect. household app. Market elasticity: 0.5; No. of sub-industries 1

	Argentina	Brazil	Uruguay	ROL	ROW
No. of *firms*	12.00	18.00	6.00	36.00	150.00
Average firm[a]	29.83	103.97	5.00	62.76	62.93
Production[a]	358.00	1871.40	30.00	2259.40	9438.81
Consumption[a]	360.95	1842.58	31.18	2279.19	9443.70
Herfindahl index	0.240	0.166	0.395	0.078	0.020
ROW tariffs[b]	25.00	55.00	35.00	38.00	
Tariff reduction[b]					
Argentina	0.00	50.00	25.00	10.00	0.00
Brazil	50.00	0.00	25.00	10.00	0.00
Uruguay	75.00	50.00	0.00	10.00	0.00
ROL	10.00	10.00	10.00	0.00	0.00
ROW	0.00	0.00	0.00	0.00	0.00
Shares in production[b]					
Argentina	98.85	0.04	0.64	0.23	0.24
Brazil	0.06	0.05	98.11	0.36	1.41
Uruguay	7.51	92.31	0.07	0.07	0.05
ROL	0.01	0.00	0.00	97.60	2.39
ROW	0.04	0.02	0.04	0.70	99.19

MOS[a] 62.76; increase in average costs at 1/2 output per model 10 %, at 1/2 number of models 5 %; linear/loglinear weights 0.5, 0.5

[a] million USD, [b] percentages , [c] from MERCOSUR average

Table A19 (cont.). Simulation of trade liberalization. Basic data and parameters

ISIC 3843-Motor vehicles. Market elasticity: 0.5; No. of sub-industries: 1

	Argentina	Brazil	Uruguay	ROL	ROW
No. of firms	5.00	7.00	4.00	8.00	39.00
Average firm[a]	631.00	2328.57	17.83	1220.39	1224.03
Production[a]	3155.00	16300.00	71.31	9763.16	47737.21
Consumption[a]	3268.11	15225.58	94.09	11409.83	47029.06
Herfindahl index	0.176	0.139	0.134	0.083	0.024
ROW tariffs[b]	35.00	60.00	40.00	45.00	
Tariff reduction[b]					
Argentina	0.00	40.00	30.00	10.00	0.00
Brazil	40.00	0.00	30.00	10.00	0.00
Uruguay	75.00	50.00	0.00	10.00	0.00
ROL	10.00	10.00	10.00	0.00	0.00
ROW	0.00	0.00	0.00	0.00	0.00
Shares in production[b]					
Argentina	97.15	1.07	0.12	0.85	0.80
Brazil	0.21	92.17	0.11	1.30	6.21
Uruguay	3.39	0.03	94.81	0.03	1.75
ROL	0.12	0.17	0.00	94.82	4.89
ROW	0.32	0.32	0.01	4.01	95.34

MOS[a] 1220.39; increase in average costs at 2 output per model -10%, at 2 number of models -5%; linear/loglinear weights 0.5, 0.5

[a] million USD, [b] percentages , [c] from MERCOSUR average

Table A20. Simulation of trade liberalization. Calibration results

ISIC 3513-Artificial and synthetic fibers.

	Argentina	Brazil	Uruguay	ROL
	Bertrand calibration *Product group elasticity: 8.74*			
Model number	25.00	115.00	8.00	71.00
Model conjectures[b]	25.31	25.71	24.90	25.63
Preference foreign products[b]	57.95	97.45	12.55	96.45
Price index[b]	1.32	1.01	1.77	0.99
Profitability deviations[c]				
Million USD	-6.09	13.46	-3.16	-4.20
as % of sales	-2.18	0.71	-9.88	-0.19
Gov. tariff revenue[a]	21.96	96.43	3.99	0.00
Tariff equivalents[b]				
Argentina	0.00	48.00	49.00	24.00
Brazil	53.00	0.00	59.00	40.00
Uruguay	18.00	20.00	0.00	58.00
ROL	51.00	67.00	66.00	0.00
	Cournot calibration *Product group elasticity 23.22*			
	Argentina	Brazil	Uruguay	ROL
Model number	25.00	118.00	7.00	77.00
Model conjectures[b]	-2.14	-2.16	-2.00	-2.23
Preference foreign products[b]	99.25	99.96	13.67	99.96
Price index[b]	1.12	0.96	1.57	0.90
Profitability deviations[c]				
Million USD	9.01	55.40	2.14	-66.55
as % of sales	3.22	2.94	6.69	-3.03
Gov. tariff revenue[a]	21.96	96.43	3.99	0.00
Tariff equivalents[b]				
Argentina	0.00	27.00	46.00	12.00
Brazil	35.00	0.00	51.00	21.00
Uruguay	17.00	13.00	0.00	26.00
ROL	34.00	39.00	55.00	0.00

[a] million USD, [b] percentages , [c] from MERCOSUR average

Table A20 (cont.). Simulation of trade liberalization. Calibration results

ISIC 3522-Pharmaceutical products.

Bertrand calibration
Product group elasticity: 4.77

	Argentina	Brazil	Uruguay	ROL
Model number	26.00	45.00	5.00	32.00
Model conjectures[b]	16.83	16.86	16.76	16.90
Preference foreign products[b]	1.03	3.48	0.61	12.23
Price index[b]	1.78	1.41	3.33	1.24
Profitability deviations[c]				
Million USD	-1.08	55.68	-30.14	-24.46
as % of sales	-0.09	1.81	-25.86	-0.55
Gov. tariff revenue[a]	10.77	49.68	5.15	0.00
Tariff equivalents[b]				
Argentina	0.00	92.00	82.00	72.00
Brazil	81.00	0.00	88.00	76.00
Uruguay	86.00	85.00	0.00	70.00
ROL	90.00	82.00	93.00	0.00

Cournot calibration
Product group elasticity 6.29

	Argentina	Brazil	Uruguay	ROL
Model number	26.00	47.00	4.00	34.00
Model conjectures[b]	-1.82	-1.84	-1.77	-1.86
Preference foreign products[b]	0.74	4.55	0.29	17.47
Price index[b]	1.51	1.23	2.63	1.06
Profitability deviations[c]				
Million USD	53.24	100.77	-15.73	-138.28
as % of sales	4.25	3.28	-13.49	-3.11
Gov. tariff revenue[a]	10.77	49.68	5.15	0.00
Tariff equivalents[b]				
Argentina	0.00	84.00	76.00	60.00
Brazil	73.00	0.00	82.00	65.00
Uruguay	77.00	76.00	0.00	58.00
ROL	83.00	73.00	88.00	0.00

[a] million USD, [b] percentages , [c] from MERCOSUR average

Table A20 (cont.). Simulation of trade liberalization. Calibration results

ISIC 3691-Bricks and other clay products.

	Bertrand calibration *Product group elasticity: 5.77*			
	Argentina	Brazil	Uruguay	ROL
Model number	4.00	55.00	1.00	20.00
Model conjectures[b]	-2.21	-2.21	-2.21	-2.21
Preference foreign products[b]	23.23	78.49	5.17	75.63
Price index[b]	1.48	0.98	2.94	0.94
Profitability deviations[c]				
Million USD	-0.14	3.85	0.01	-3.72
as % of sales	-0.08	0.25	0.10	-0.21
Gov. tariff revenue[a]	9.04	16.33	0.43	0.00
Tariff equivalents[b]				
Argentina	0.00	83.00	73.00	72.00
Brazil	75.00	0.00	74.00	59.00
Uruguay	39.00	36.00	0.00	47.00
ROL	89.00	91.00	89.00	0.00
	Cournot calibration *Product group elasticity 6.95*			
	Argentina	Brazil	Uruguay	ROL
Model number	4.00	54.00	1.00	21.00
Model conjectures[b]	-2.20	-2.17	-2.19	-2.21
Preference foreign products[b]	28.45	89.62	5.51	87.29
Price index[b]	1.37	1.01	2.59	0.94
Profitability deviations[c]				
Million USD	-1.28	36.22	0.04	-34.99
as % of sales	-0.72	2.33	0.76	-2.01
Gov. tariff revenue[a]	9.04	16.33	0.43	0.00
Tariff equivalents[b]				
Argentina	0.00	78.00	69.00	65.00
Brazil	68.00	0.00	69.00	52.00
Uruguay	35.00	35.00	0.00	41.00
ROL	84.00	86.00	85.00	0.00

[a] million USD, [b] percentages , [c] from MERCOSUR average

Table A20 (cont.). Simulation of trade liberalization. Calibration results

ISIC 3825-Office machinery.

	Bertrand calibration *Product group elasticity 9.53*			
	Argentina	Brazil	Uruguay	ROL
Model number	33.00	58.00	0.00	45.00
Model conjectures[b]	48.15	48.27	46.96	48.22
Preference foreign products[b]	56.20	97.15	4.08	94.32
Price index[b]	1.20	1.03	2.09	0.98
Profitability deviations[c]				
Million USD	-2.46	24.48	-19.42	-2.60
as % of sales	-1.50	0.99	-751.86	-0.10
Gov. tariff revenue[a]	25.16	173.99	3.06	0.00
Tariff equivalents[b]				
Argentina	0.00	46.00	53.00	23.00
Brazil	36.00	0.00	63.00	37.00
Uruguay	26.00	38.00	0.00	38.00
ROL	39.00	57.00	67.00	0.00
	Cournot calibration *Product group elasticity 12.48*			
	Argentina	Brazil	Uruguay	ROL
Model number	33.00	57.00	0.00	45.00
Model conjectures[b]	2.21	2.22	2.09	2.22
Preference foreign products[b]	54.54	99.54	8.37	98.30
Price index[b]	1.21	1.03	1.77	0.98
Profitability deviations[c]				
Million USD	-2.80	46.14	-19.46	-23.88
as % of sales	-1.70	1.86	-753.29	-0.90
Gov. tariff revenue[a]	25.16	173.99	3.06	0.00
Tariff equivalents[b]				
Argentina	0.00	40.00	46.00	19.00
Brazil	34.00	0.00	55.00	31.00
Uruguay	25.00	31.00	0.00	29.00
ROL	36.00	49.00	58.00	0.00

[a] million USD, [b] percentages , [c] from MERCOSUR average

Table A20 (cont.). Simulation of trade liberalization. Calibration results

SIC 3831-part- Electrical power machinery

	Argentina	Brazil	Uruguay	ROL
	Bertrand calibration *Product group elasticity 6.33*			
Model number	6.00	45.00	0.00	26.00
Model conjectures[b]	32.46	33.05	31.55	32.89
Preference foreign products[b]	12.94	75.41	9.16	83.63
Price index[b]	1.71	1.04	2.77	0.93
Profitability deviations[c]				
Million USD	-26.52	54.95	-23.28	-5.15
as % of sales	-13.26	1.74	-261.10	-0.15
Gov. tariff revenue[a]	23.54	219.44	2.96	0.00
Tariff equivalents[b]				
Argentina	0.00	51.00	54.00	46.00
Brazil	73.00	0.00	69.00	55.00
Uruguay	43.00	10.00	0.00	47.00
ROL	82.00	77.00	89.00	0.00
	Cournot calibration *Product group elasticity 6.74*			
	Argentina	Brazil	Uruguay	ROL
Model number	6.00	45.00	0.00	27.00
Model conjectures[b]	4.43	4.53	4.27	4.50
Preference foreign products[b]	12.22	77.50	9.66	86.26
Price index[b]	1.65	1.02	2.56	0.91
Profitability deviations[c]				
Million USD	-23.49	71.81	-22.97	-25.35
as % of sales	-11.74	2.28	-257.66	-0.75
Gov. tariff revenue[a]	23.54	219.44	2.96	0.00
Tariff equivalents[b]				
Argentina	0.00	49.00	52.00	44.00
Brazil	71.00	0.00	66.00	52.00
Uruguay	42.00	11.00	0.00	44.00
ROL	81.00	75.00	88.00	0.00

[a] million USD, [b] percentages , [c] from MERCOSUR average

Table A20 (cont.). Simulation of trade liberalization. Calibration results

ISIC 3833-29-part- Electrical household appliances

Bertrand calibration
Product group elasticity 9.48

	Argentina	Brazil	Uruguay	ROL
Model number	30.00	110.00	5.00	66.00
Model conjectures[b]	48.73	48.70	49.30	48.04
Preference foreign products[b]	33.90	97.61	5.29	92.11
Price index[b]	1.27	0.98	1.87	0.96
Profitability deviations[c]				
Million USD	-4.56	26.00	-7.09	-14.35
as % of sales	-1.27	1.39	-23.63	-0.64
Gov. tariff revenue[a]	1.86	8.60	2.10	0.00
Tariff equivalents[b]				
Argentina	0.00	40.00	63.00	46.00
Brazil	60.00	0.00	64.00	46.00
Uruguay	21.00	50.00	0.00	49.00
ROL	69.00	74.00	77.00	0.00

Cournot calibration
Product group elasticity 19.63

	Argentina	Brazil	Uruguay	ROL
Model number	30.00	114.00	4.00	71.00
Model conjectures[b]	-2.63	-2.40	-3.09	-2.32
Preference foreign products[b]	42.58	99.99	17.81	99.99
Price index[b]	1.12	0.93	1.53	0.88
Profitability deviations[c]				
Million USD	14.10	55.78	-3.56	-66.33
as % of sales	3.94	2.98	-11.85	-2.94
Gov. tariff revenue[a]	1.86	8.60	2.10	0.00
Tariff equivalents[b]				
Argentina	0.00	25.00	51.00	26.00
Brazil	44.00	0.00	53.00	28.00
Uruguay	17.00	28.00	0.00	25.00
ROL	49.00	50.00	62.00	0.00

[a] million USD, [b] percentages , [c] from MERCOSUR average

Table A20 (cont.). Simulation of trade liberalization. Calibration results

ISIC 3843-Motor vehicles

	Bertrand calibration *Product group elasticity 6.25*			
	Argentina	Brazil	Uruguay	ROL
Model number	631.00	2470.00	15.00	1274.00
Model conjectures[b]	50.41	49.52	51.53	49.40
Preference foreign products[b]	30.98	95.68	1.63	93.43
Price index[b]	1.34	0.92	3.04	0.96
Profitability deviations[c]				
Million USD	-118.09	421.38	-239.40	-63.89
as % of sales	-3.74	2.59	-335.71	-0.65
Gov. tariff revenue[a]	124.97	409.92	13.94	0.00
Tariff equivalents[b]				
Argentina	0.00	50.00	75.00	52.00
Brazil	70.00	0.00	77.00	51.00
Uruguay	37.00	71.00	0.00	70.00
ROL	71.00	63.00	92.00	0.00

	Cournot calibration *Product group elasticity 8.53*			
	Argentina	Brazil	Uruguay	ROL
Model number	631.00	2522.00	16.00	1331.00
Model conjectures[b]	4.24	3.99	4.54	3.95
Preference foreign products[b]	41.57	99.67	2.42	98.81
Price index[b]	1.23	0.91	2.24	0.92
Profitability deviations[c]				
Million USD	-40.10	491.35	-232.86	-218.39
as % of sales	-1.27	3.01	-326.55	-2.24
Gov. tariff revenue[a]	124.97	409.92	13.94	0.00
Tariff equivalents[b]				
Argentina	0.00	41.00	66.00	41.00
Brazil	61.00	0.00	68.00	42.00
Uruguay	30.00	58.00	0.00	56.00
ROL	62.00	53.00	85.00	0.00

[a] million USD, [b] percentages , [c] from MERCOSUR average

References

Abd-el Rahman, K. (1991): Firms Competitive and National Comparative Advantages as Joint Determinants of Trade Composition. Weltwirtschatfliches Archiv 127, 83-97

Aquino, A. (1978): Intra-Industry Trade and Inter-Industry Specialization as Concurrent Sources of International Trade in Manufactures. Weltwirtschafliches Archiv 114, 275-296

Baumann, R. (1989): Los Bienes de Capital y la Integración entre Brasil y Argentina. Integración Latinoamericana, 152, 3-13

Behar, J. (1980): Una Interpretación Crítica de la Integración Latinoamericana. Comercio Exterior, 30, 423-432

Behar, J. (1991): Economic Integration and Intra-Industry Trade: The Case of the Argentine-Brazilian Free Trade Agreement. Journal of Common Markets Studies, 29, 527-552

Behar, J. (1994): Trade and Economies of Scale in Mercosur Countries. Research Reports 69. Institute of Latin American Studies, Stockholm

Behar, J. (1995): Measuring the Effects of Economic Integration for the Southern-Cone Countries. Industry Simulations of Trade Liberalization. Journal of Developing Areas 33, 3-31

Behar, J. (1996): Plant-size Effects of Trade: The Case of MERCOSUR Countries. In: Karlsson, W., Malaki, A. (Eds.): Growth, Trade and Integration in Latin America. Institute of Latin American Studies, Stockholm

Behar, J. (1997): The MERCOSUR Pattern of Intra-Industry Trade, Research Reports 75. Institute of Latin American Studies, Stockholm

Berlinski, J. et al. (1984): Importaciones Exentas de Aranceles en Algunos Países de ALADI. BID-INTAL, Buenos Aires

BID-INTAL (1985): Estadísticas del Intercambio Comercial de los Países Latinoamericanos 1980-84. BID-INTAL, Buenos Aires

Brander, J.A. (1981): Intra-Industry Trade in Identical Commodities. Journal of International Economics 11, 1-14

Buxedas, M., Roca, J (1984): Concentración en la Industria Manufacturera. Resultados de las Mediciones de la Concentración y Algunas Conclusiones Primarias. CIEDUR, Montevideo

Calvo, G. A., Végh, C. A. (1994): Inflation, Stabilization and Nominal Anchors. Contemporary Economic Policy 12

Caves, R.E. (1981): Intra-Industry Trade and Market Structure in the Industrial Countries. Oxford Economic Papers 33, 203-23.

ECLAC (various years): Anuario Estadístico de América Latina. ECLAC, Santiago

Chudnovsky, D. (1985): South-South Trade in Capital Goods. The Experiences of Argentina and Brazil. CET/IPAL, Buenos Aires

Cline, W.R. (1982): Economies of Scale and Economic Integration in Latin America. In Conesa, E., Nuñez del Arco, J. (Eds.): Terms of Trade and the Optimum Tariff in Latin America, pp 233-77. IDB-INTAL, Buenos Aires

Drabek, Z., Greenaway, D. (1984): Economic Integration and Intra-Industry Trade: the CMEA and EC Compared. Kyklos 37, 444-469

Eaton, B.C. and Lipsey, R. G. (1989): Product Differentiation. In R. Schmalensee and R. D. Willig (Eds.): Handbook of Industrial Organization, pp. 723-68, Amsterdam, North Holland

Eaton, J. and Kierzkowski, H. (1984): Oligopolistic Competition, Product Variety, and International Trade. In H. Kierzkowski, (ed.), Monopolistic Competition and International Trade, pp. 69-83, Oxford, Oxford University Press

Erzan, R. and Laird, S. (1984): Intra-industry Trade of Developing Countries and Some Policy Issues. Discussion Papers No 12, Geneva, UNCTAD

Ethier, W. (1979): Internationally Decreasing Costs and World Trade. Journal of International Economics, 9, pp. 1-24

Ethier, W.J. (1982): Decreasing Costs in International Trade and Frank Grahams Argument for Protection. Econometrica, 50, pp. 1242-68

Falvey, R.E. (1981): Commercial Policy and Intra-Industry Trade. Journal of International Economics, 11, pp. 495-511

Falvey, R.E. and Kierzkowsky, H. (1987): Product Quality, Intra-Industry Trade and (Im)perfect Competition. In H. Kierzkowski (ed.), Protection and Competition in International Trade, pp. 143-61, Oxford,:Basil Blackwell

Gasiorek, M., Smith, A. and A. Venables (1989): Tariffs, Subsidies and Retaliation. European Economic Review, 33, 480-490

Gray, P. H. (1988): Intra-Industry Trade: An Untidy Phenomenom. Weltwirtschatfliches Archiv, 124, pp. 211-227

Greenaway, D. and Milner, C.R. (1986): The Economics of Intra-Industry Trade (Oxford: Basil Blackwel)

Greenaway, D. T. (1989): Regional Trading Arrangements and Intra-Industry Trade: Evidence and Policy Issues. In D.T Greenaway, T. Hyclak, and R.J Thornton (Eds.): Economic Aspects of Regional Trading Arrangements pp 31-42, New York, Harvester Wheatsheaf

Grubel, H.G and P.J. Lloyd (Eds.) (1975): Intra-Industry Trade: The Theory and Measurement of International Trade in Differentiated Products, London, Macmillan

Gual, J., Martínez-Giralt, X. and Vives, X. (1989): Spain in the EC: the impact of trade liberalization on selected industries (Conference Papper)

Helg, R. and Ranci, P. (1988): Economies of Scale and the Integration of the European Economy: the Case of Italy. In Research of the Costs of Non-Europe, Basic Findings. Studies on the Economics of Integration, 2, pp. 204-285. Commission of the European Communities

Helpman, E. and Krugman, P.R. (1989): Trade Policy and Market Structure, Cambridge, Mass.:MIT Press

Hodges, M. and Wallace, W. (Eds.) (1981): Economic Divergence in the European Community, London, Boston, Sydney, George Allen & Unwin

IDB (Annual): Economic and Social Progress in Latin American Economic Integration

IDB/IRELA (1996): Foreign Direct Investment in Latin America in the 1990s, Madrid, Authors

Jacobsson, S. (1988): Intra-Industry Specialization and Development Models for the Capital Goods Sector. Weltwirtschaftliches Archiv, 124, pp. 14-37

Kol, J. and Rayment, P. (1989): Allyn Young Specialisation and Intermediate Goods in Intra-Industry Trade. In P.K.M.Tharakan and J. Kol (Eds.): Intra-Industry Trade. Theory, Evidence and Extensions, pp. 51-68, London. The Macmillan Press Ltd

Krugman, P.R. (1981): Intraindustry Specialization and the Gains from Trade. Journal of Political Economy, 89, pp. 959-73

Krugman, P.R. (1989): Industrial Organization and International Trade. In Schmalensee, W. and R.D. Willig (eds), Handbook of Industrial Organization, pp 1179-1224, Amsterdam, North Holland

Krugman, P. R. (1990): Rethinking International Trade, Cambridge, Mass., MIT Press

Lancaster, K. (1984): Protection and Product Differentiation. In H. Kierzkowski (ed.), Monopolistic Competition and International Trade, pp. 137-56, Oxford, Oxford University Press

Lord, M. (1992): Latin Americas Exports of Manufactured Goods. In IDB (Eds.): Economic and Social Progress in Latin America. 1992 Report, Washington, D.C., The Johns Hopkins University Press

Müller, J. and Owen, N. (1985): The effects of trade on plant size. In Joachim Schwalbach (ed.), Industry Structure and Performance. Berlin, WZB., pp. 41-60

Norman, V. (1989): EFTA and the internal European market. Economic Policy, 9, 424-465

Norman, V (1990): Assessing Trade and Welfare Effects of Trade Liberalization. European Economic Review, 34, pp. 725-51

Patrickson, A. (1990): Essays in the Latin American Fertilizer Industry. Studies in International Economics and Geography N 10, Stockholm: Stockholm School of Economics

Pomfret, R. (1979): Intra-Industry Trade in International Trade. In H. Giersch (ed.), On the Economics of Intra Industry Trade, pp. 115.31, Tubingen,J.C.B. Mohr

Pratten, C.F. (1975): Economies of Scale in Manufacturing Industries, Cambridge, Cambridge University Press

Pratten, C.F. (1988): A Survey of the Economies of Scales. In Research of the Costs of Non-Europe, Basic Findings. Studies on the Economics of Integration, 2, pp. 11-164. Commission of the European Communities

Pratten, C. F. (1991): Economies of Scale and Latin American Exports. In: Hugh, H. Schwartz (ed.), Supply and Marketing Constraints on Latin American Manufacturing Exports, pp. 61-86, Washington, D.C., IDB

Reynolds, C.W et al. (1993): A Case for Open Regionalism in the Andes. Policy Implications of Andean Integration in a Period of Hemispheric Liberalization and Structural Adjustment. Report for USAID/ILDIS-Friedrich Ebert

Richardson, J.D (1989): Empirical Research on Trade Liberalization with Imperfect Competition: A Survey. OECD Economic Studies, 12, pp. 7-50

Rosenberg, N. (1976): Perspectives on Technology, Cambridge, Cambridge University Press

Scherer, F. M. et al. (1975): The Economics of Multi-Plant Operation: An International Comparisons Study. Cambridge, Mass., Harvard University Press

Scherer, F. M. and Ross, D. (1990): Industrial Market Structure and Economic Performance. Boston, Houghton Mifflin Cop

Schwalbach, J. (1988): Economies of Scale and Intra-Community Trade. In Research of the Costs of Non-Europe, Basic Findings. Studies on the Economics of Integration, 2, pp. 166-204. Commission of the European Communities

Smith, A. and Venables, A. (1988): Completing the internal market in the European Community. European Economic Review, 32, 1501-1525

Tharakan, P.K.M. (1986): The Intra-Industry Trade of Benelux with the Developing World. Weltwirtschaftliches Archiv, 122, pp. 131-149

UNIDO (1993): Trade Integration and Industrial Restructuring: The Case of MERCOSUR, PPD.235(SPEC). Vienna, Author

UN (1986): Classification by Broad Economic Categories, Statistical Papers, Series M, N 53, Rev. 2. New York, Author

Venables, A.J. (1987a): Customs Union and Tariff Reform Under Imperfect Competition. European Economic Review, 31, pp. 103-110

Venables, A.J. (1987b): Trade and Trade Policy with Differentiated Products: A Chamberlinian- Ricardian Model. The Economic Journal, 97, pp. 700-17

Wonnacott, P. (1987): The United States and Canada: The Quest for Free Trade. an Examination of Selected Issues. Policy Analyses in International Economics No. 16. Institute for International Economics, Washington D.C.

Index

Argentina, 2, 4, 9-10, 16-18, 20-33, 37-39, 41, 44-47, 49-53, 57, 59-62, 67-69, 72, 77, 80-84, 88-94, 96-102, 105, 107-108, 110, 112-113, 116-118, 120
Bolivia, 2, 104-105, 107, 110, 116-119
Brazil, 2, 4, 9-10, 16-18, 20-25, 27-33, 37-39, 41, 44-47, 49-53, 57, 59-63, 65-69, 77, 80-84, 86, 88-102, 107, 110, 113, 116-120

capital goods, 9-10, 14-15, 18-19, 23-25, 28, 34, 41, 51, 62, 66-67, 114
CARICOM, 104
Chile, 2, 4, 104, 105, 107
Colombia, 104, 105, 107, 116-119
comparative advantage, 16-17, 22, 28, 67
competition, 4-7, 9, 11-14, 27-29, 47, 49, 57-59, 66-67, 77-78, 85, 88-89, 94-96, 102, 104, 105, 113
    Bertrand behavior, 49, 69, 71, 74, 76-83, 87, 89, 90, 97-100
    Cournot behavior, 69, 71, 75-79, 89-93
    imperfect, 7, 13-14, 28-29, 49, 78
    monopolistic, 12-14
    oligopolistic, 11
consumer goods, 5, 14, 18, 20-21, 34, 41, 52, 65-66
cooperation, 2, 4-6, 9
    economic, 2, 4, 9
    monetary, 9
cost
    average, 29, 50, 59, 75, 85, 88-89, 95-96
    efficiency, 6, 51, 57, 66

divergences
    in economic structure, 29
    in external performance, 119-120
    in growth rates, 117
    in income per capita, 117
    in monetary conditions, 97-100, 102, 110-111
    in tariffs, 95, 105

economic efficiency, 6, 46, 56
economic integration, 1-7, 10-12, 21, 26-29, 32, 36, 38, 49-50, 51, 52, 67, 69, 77, 84, 88, 95-97, 101-107, 109, 112, 114, 116, 118-120
    customs union, 2, 3, 7, 11-12, 77, 90, 94, 95, 102-103, 105, 113
    free trade area, 1, 80, 116, 119
economic interdependence, 4, 101, 103, 106, 108-109, 118
economies of scale, 6, 7, 9, 12, 14-16, 24, 26, 27, 29, 38, 41, 46, 50-52, 57, 67, 69-70, 88, 101
Ecuador, 105, 107, 116- 119

firm size, 72

GRAN, 103-113, 115-120

inter-industry
    adjustment, 7, 16, 18, 27, 84
    specialization, 20-21, 34, 36, 39, 40, 50, 52
    trade, 11-12, 28
intermediate goods, 5, 14, 18, 22-23, 25, 28, 41, 45
intra-firm trade, 11, 48
intra-industry
    indices, 18-19, 22, 35-36, 41, 47, 52

specialization, 7, 11-13, 15, 19, 28-29, 38-39, 48, 51-52
trade, 9, 11-16, 18-24, 27-28, 30, 34, 36-42, 45-52
investments, 5, 7, 24, 57, 78, 108
large scale, 5, 7, 57

labor productivity, 59, 60
LAFTA, 1, 116
LAIA, 1, 2, 10, 30, 37, 39, 46-47, 49, 52, 70, 72, 75-77, 79-83, 85, 90-93, 97-101, 104, 107-108

market
concentration, 6, 47, 59, 61, 66, 76, 101
shares, 53, 57, 59, 67, 95-96
size, 26-28, 59-60, 62, 65-66, 78, 88
MERCOSUR, 1, 2, 5, 7, 29-33, 36-40, 42-43, 45, 47-49, 51-52, 67, 69-70, 72, 76-85, 87, 89-95, 97-113, 116-120
Mexico, 2, 24, 39, 77, 104, 107-108
minimum efficient scale, 16, 51, 53, 55-57, 59-60, 72, 77-78, 88
minimum optimal scale, 24-28

NAFTA, 2, 104

Paraguay, 2, 4, 30-32, 37, 39, 41, 44, 45-47, 51, 70, 84, 107, 112-113, 116-120
Peru, 104, 107, 110, 111, 113-114, 116-118
PICEAB, 9-12, 20, 25, 28, 32
plant size, 7, 52, 51-53, 55, 57, 59-60, 65-68
policy coordination, 4, 94, 96
product differentiation, 9, 11, 13-16, 18, 22-24, 28-29, 36, 40-41, 51, 52, 71, 76, 89
horizontal, 15-16, 36-39, 42, 52
vertical, 16, 39, 42, 52
product variety, 13, 14, 15, 16, 19

tariff
barriers, 1, 28, 48, 80, 85, 90, 101
common, 51, 90, 94, 95, 102, 105, 115
differential, 18, 101
external, 2, 10, 51, 94, 97-100, 104
reduction, 6, 10, 13, 50, 51, 69, 79-81, 84-85, 89-91, 100-101
trade liberalization, 1, 2, 5, 6, 7, 9, 11-14, 16, 18-20, 27-28, 38, 51, 56, 77, 80, 88-89, 101, 103-105, 119

Uruguay, 2, 4, 30-33, 37-39, 41, 43-46, 48-53, 57, 60-61, 63-67, 69, 77, 80-84, 88-102, 107-108, 112-113, 116-120

vertical specialization, 15, 22-23, 41

Druck: Strauss Offsetdruck, Mörlenbach
Verarbeitung: Schäffer, Grünstadt